The Babysitting Bible

The Babysitting Bible

Jordan Lane

Writers Club Press
San Jose New York Lincoln Shanghai

The Babysitting Bible

Writers Club Press
an imprint of iUniverse, Inc.

For information address:
iUniverse, Inc.
5220 S. 16th St., Suite 200
Lincoln, NE 68512
www.iuniverse.com

ISBN: 0-595-24658-3

Printed in the United States of America

This book is dedicated to my family, to Amy and babysitters everywhere.

There are only two lasting bequests we can hope to give our children. One of these is roots, the other, wings.

—Hodding Carter, Pulitzer Prize winning writer

Contents

Introduction

So you want to be a babysitter. Great! Babysitting is one of the most popular jobs for young people today. It teaches you how to be responsible, mature, and a well-rounded individual. Before you march out the door on the way to your first job you will need to know a few things. That is where this book is helpful. Within these pages you will learn what you can expect from children of different ages, how to find and keep your jobs, how to have fun on the job by playing games inside and outside, as well as answering any questions and concerns that you may have. You will also learn how to deal with problems as well as other useful and life saving tips, topics, and tidbits.

Babysitting is one of the most common jobs for teenaged girls and boys. (Boys can be just as good a babysitter as girls.) It is challenging, entertaining, memorable and above all, rewarding. In order to become a successful babysitter, it helps to know a few secrets and tips. This book will teach you how to not only become a good babysitter, but will teach you how to become a GREAT babysitter. You will soon become a better and more profitable babysitter who will have more jobs than you can possibly imagine.

The definition of babysitting in the dictionary is "to provide care for a child in the absence of a parent or guardian." It is your job to take care of children without any parental supervision. This is a very important job for which you need to be prepared before you do it. This book will prepare you to babysit.

Babysitting is more than just caring for children as the dictionary defines it. Babysitting offers the opportunity where you can learn numerous valuable skills that will help you throughout your life.

Babysitting also is an opportunity where you can earn some money. Most importantly babysitting offers an opportunity for you to meet new people who could be friends of yours for a very long time. You must take babysitting seriously in order to be a great babysitter. This is where *The Babysitting Bible* enters the picture.

This book, *The Babysitting Bible*, will teach you what makes a great babysitter. You will learn many skills, games, and how to respond to many different situations. This book contains ten chapters, an introduction, conclusion and a section at the end where you can write down any important information such as families' names, phone numbers, notes about your babysitting jobs, and anything else. We will now briefly review each informative chapter. The first chapter is entitled "Kid Types." This chapter explores different types of children and how they develop, act, grow, and learn. "What Parents Look For In A Babysitter," is the title of chapter two. This chapter offers you hints and suggestions as to what parents are attempting to find when they search for a babysitter. The information in this chapter will give you a head start to impressing the parents of the kids who you will be babysitting as well as offering suggestions and hints to enhance your chances of finding babysitting jobs.

Chapter three is entitled "Am I Ready To Babysit?" This chapter gives you a sense of what is involved in babysitting and how to tell if you are ready. The fourth chapter is called "How To Start Babysitting." It explains the various ways that you can find babysitting jobs. This chapter explores different places, people, and organizations that may help you acquire jobs. Chapter five is named "Starting Your First Job…And How To Keep It." This section describes what is expected of you and what you should do when you start a babysitting job for the first time. This chapter also gives you hints on how to impress the parents and the kids so they will ask you back over and over again to babysit. Chapter six is entitled "Having Fun On The Job." This chapter explains one of the most important aspects of babysitting, having fun. You will learn games that you can play inside and outside as well as learning different safety and playtime rules.

"What To Do And Not To Do While Babysitting" is the seventh chapter. This crucial chapter goes over what is appropriate for babysitting and what is inappropriate. You will learn how you should and should not act and the consequences of doing a poor job. Chapter eight is entitled "What About…" This chapter reviews serious questions and topics that will come up as you babysit. Some examples of important topics and questions answered in this chapter are: What About Baths? and What About Bedtime? just to name a couple. Chapter nine is called "Just For Parents." This chapter explores topics that parents need to know about babysitting and babysitters. If the parents are organized then your babysitting job will go much smoother. Chapter ten is entitled "Important Stuff." It is here that you learn about first aid and what to do in an emergency. This chapter is brimmed with useful information that could save your life or the lives of children you are babysitting.

As you can tell this book is designed to make you the best babysitter in the world. You will learn how to handle any situation regardless of how serious it may be. You will learn first aid, how to deal with children and their parents, how to play games and many other useful skills that can be used for the rest of your life. I hope you enjoy reading this book as much as I did writing it. Welcome to the world of babysitting!

Chapter One

Kid Types

Babysitting is like any other job; you need to know what you are doing before you start working. If you are a dentist, you need to know about teeth. If you are a babysitter, you need to know about children. So before you take your first babysitting job, you need to know that there are six general categories in which most kids fit. But kids, like you and me, are all unique so these categories might not fit the children you are babysitting exactly, but they are close.

The different categories of children are Oozers, Wigglers & Gigglers, Walkers & Talkers, Gamers, Independents and Older Kids. These different categories can be used as a guide to what you might expect with different aged children.

Oozers

Oozers range from ages 0-2. They need the most attention of any age group. Oozers are basically helpless babies that need you for everything. However, development comes very quickly. In fact, they change more than any other group. For example, when oozers are a few months old they will attempt to rollover on their back or stomachs. Then they will attempt to sit up around four or five months old. Once the little ones get that down, they will begin to scoot across the ground and then will crawl. By the time oozers are around a year old or so (it is different for every toddler) they will start to walk and then they are off to the races, running by the time they are two years old. Oozers also go through other changes. For example, they get teeth.

You will notice tiny teeth protruding through their gums. When kids this age are teething, their mouths may be sore and they will cry for what seems like no reason, but it could be because of the tiny sharp teeth pushing their way out through the tender gums. You probably will not remember what that feels like, but it hurts!

Oozers also struggle to communicate with sounds and slight motions. If they want something you might see them wave their arms around and produce gurgling sounds. If oozers don't get what they want they could start to fuss or cry. If you find an oozer struggling to communicate with you, be patient. Attempt to find out what they could possibly want by offering them common items they are used to such as a bottle or a favorite toy, for example. If you can't figure out what they want, don't worry. They may just be making sounds to be heard.

Oozers also put anything and everything in their mouth. They do this not because they are hungry, but because they want to explore their environment. Instead of using their eyes and hands like we do, oozers put things in their mouths to check them out. When you are playing with or holding an oozer, watch out. They may try to put your jewelry, hair, and anything else in their mouth. Keep the play area clear of things that they may put into their mouths, especially if there are small items on which the child may choke. Also, many oozers have small, sharp fingernails that can easily scratch you if you are not careful. Be especially careful that they do not scratch your eyes.

Much of your time with oozers will be spent holding them. When you do hold them you need to do it carefully and always support their bodies and especially their heads. If you do not know how to hold a baby correctly, ask their parents to show you. Generally you want to hold a baby close to your body, supporting their entire body anyway that you can. Babies this age can be very active and can be the most entertaining and difficult age group to deal with. They need diapers, bottles, naps, burping, constant vigil, and tremendous patience on your part. These kids need total attention and can be very frustrating. They can cry for hours at a time without giving any clue to what they might want. Oozers can also spit up their food all over you and wet their diapers without warning.

On the other hand, this age group is quite special. They will hold your fingers with their tiny hands, which can be a rewarding and cute experience. Holding oozers correctly in your arms can also be very rewarding and give you a special feeling. But, it is a fact that they will be seeping liquids from any and all holes in their body. That's why they are called oozers. They may spit up, have a runny nose and, of course, need their diapers changed (which is discussed in chapter eight).

When dealing with oozers ensure you always keep an eye on them. If they are not in a safe area like a crib, play area or a safe place on the floor, then they should be in your arms.

Wigglers & Gigglers

Wigglers and gigglers range from ages 2-4 and will keep you occupied. This is the time when kids begin to explore the world around them and start to form likes and dislikes. They start to move quickly, are comfortable walking, and begin to develop verbal skills. Wigglers and gigglers must always be watched or taken to a safe area where they can play. When you take a child this age to a safe play area, show them their boundaries and if they break the rules, let them know that they will need to take a time out or will receive other suitable punishments.

Children this age become more and more curious about the world around them. Wigglers and gigglers, like the oozers, put many things into their mouths. They like to draw and may draw on the kitchen walls in red crayon if you are not careful. However, they are still very dependent on you. You need to prepare food for them, bathe them, and supervise them. Youngsters this age begin to be potty trained, but not all kids this age are so you may still need to change their diapers. If you are not sure if they are potty trained, ask their parents. Some wigglers and gigglers may also use a pacifier, have a security blanket, or a favorite doll or toy.

Above all, children this age like to have fun. That is why they are called wigglers and gigglers. Play with them, hold them, and enjoy them.

Wigglers and gigglers also begin to understand the world around them a bit more then oozers. They know what they want and they are learning how to verbalize what that is. At this age children form bonds to certain items. One kid may like dolls and another may favor cars. They can play with a ball or with different toys rather contently. Give them the attention they deserve and tickle their tummy for a good laugh.

Walkers & Talkers

Walkers and talkers range from ages 4-6 and will keep you on your feet. They are well into school, books, dancing, singing, television, sports, and anything else they can reach or see. They also explore new things such as making their own food and climbing on the kitchen table. Kids this age need to be treated with more freedom than younger children but do not ignore them or a catastrophe might creep up on you. Some walkers and talkers tend to be fearless. They try to climb up on anything and experiment with all sorts of things. Walkers and talkers are little daredevils; so keep them close to you and safe at all times. Spend time talking, playing, and laughing with walkers and talkers.

Children this age are also making friends and refining interests. If they show you something they like, take the time to appreciate it and show your support for their interests. This will make your time more enjoyable, while the children will have a special time, too. Treat walkers and talkers with respect, listening to what they are saying and doing. They are developing the skills to have long and meaningful conversations. When they do talk to you at length, keep their interest; ask them questions, put forth an effort to have them think. They also understand rules at this age, so explain to them why they can not go into the street, or why they should not pull the dogs tail. The bottom line with walkers and talkers is to listen to them, talk with them, and play with them. This is an entertaining age to play with and to be with.

Gamers

Gamers range from ages 6-8 and the words here are supervised freedom. It is at this age that kids are into making friends, attending school, and playing games. They are losing their baby teeth and taking on more responsibilities such as dressing themselves, bathing themselves, and feeding themselves. Some gamers may see a babysitter as a bother, but most of them will see you as a playmate. Gamers love to play games. If they want to, by all means play with

them. Teach them new and entertaining games. If they want their freedom, allow them to play on their own but be sure they are being safe and secure. Periodic, frequent and impromptu checks on the gamers is a safe bet, even though they have developed the skills to play quietly, they can still get into trouble.

Independents

Independents range from ages 8-10 and can be a handful or a breeze, depending on the child. By this age kids have started to figure out babysitters. They know what they can and can't get away with and they know their own personal limits. Since they know their own limits they tend to be less fearless than younger kids. This can make your job easier because most independents will not try to eat paint or stuff a pile of dirt in their mouth.

For the most part, kids this age are easy to babysit. They may already be at the level where they can take care of themselves, which makes your job much easier. However, independents are at a tricky age where you need to build a good relationship with them before they have a chance figure out your weaknesses. I suggest you share your interests with them and have them share theirs with you. Attempt to become their friend. It is also at this age that you need to respect and consider the child's opinions, and allow them to come to their own decisions. (Be sure, however, that their decisions will not lead to trouble.) If you babysit a child for the first time within this age group, take some time to get to know him or her and then you can gauge how you should act towards them. But, like any kid, most independents still like to joke around and play games, so enjoy them and always remember that you are in charge.

Older Kids

Older kids range from age 10 and up and can vary greatly depending on the child. Some will be great, while others will make you work hard for your money by disagreeing with everything you say and not listening. Again, it really depends on your relationship with the youth before this point, or making a strong first impression to determine how they will respond to you. Older kids may also be fun because they may have some of the same interests that you do. Treat these kids as you would a friend, but always remember that you are the responsible adult.

Now that you have a general knowledge about different types of children and how they develop, we will now explore different personalities. Some children may exhibit more than one of these personalities. Every child will be different. The list to follow will not fit the kids you are babysitting exactly, but will give you a general idea about various personalities in children.

Spoiled kids

These kids tend to get what they want from their parents and from anyone else. Contrary to most beliefs, not all spoiled kids are brats. Some are very sweet and cooperative. However, don't expect them to be eager to clean up after themselves. When dealing with spoiled kids try not to spoil them yourself. Strive to teach them how to clean up or to do something for themselves. In most cases, it is not that spoiled kids do not want to be helpful and independent, they just don't know how to do many things.

Emotional kids

Some kids express their emotions more strongly than others do. These children tend to cry more often than other children. When they fall, for example, they carry on and on about their injury. If you babysit a child like this, be patient. When they cry you have to grin and bear it. Make sure they are not seriously hurt, and eventually they will stop crying. When some kids fall down they only cry when you see them. So when a child falls down, let them get up and brush themselves off. Chances are they are not hurt. But if they take a while to get up, then you should walk over to them to be sure they are not seriously injured.

Special needs kids

These special needs could be physical, for example they need a wheel chair, or emotional. If they have a physical need, don't be shy to discuss these needs with the child's parents or with the child. You may be surprised how open they will be. If the kid has an emotional need it might not be as obvious, chances are you may never know about it. If the parents tell you about their child's emotional situation, do your best to help the child and do what the parents tell you to do, which may include giving the child medication or other accommodations.

Average kids

These are just average, everyday kids. They like to have fun, play games, and act like any kid. Most children are average, but every kid will display some behaviors of the other types.

Smart kids

These children would rather do their homework or read a book than play a game. This is fine. If you babysit a smart kid talk to them about subjects that interest them or you. Maybe you will learn something from them or you can teach them something.

Quiet kids

Some children can be extremely quiet and shy. If you babysit one of these kids be patient. Try to talk with them and play with them. Speak in a soft tone and eventually they will like you if you are gently and patient with them. It is difficult for some kids to be left alone with a babysitter without their parents.

Active kids

Some kids have nonstop energy. They run, hide, yell, play and rarely stop. If you babysit an active child, attempt to keep up. Play games that will tire them out, or play quiet games that will calm them down.

These are just a few general examples of different types of kids and personalities that you may meet as you babysit. Remember, children can not be placed neatly into a type or category. Every child is different, every child develops at a different pace and every child will display different personality types at various times. They may be quiet one minute and boisterous the next. As you meet more and more children you will learn how to gauge what type of child they are and what they can and cannot do. Be patient and as you babysit more extensively you will become an expert with all ages and types of kids.

Chapter Two

What Parents Look For In A Babysitter

Before you start babysitting, you need to know what parents expect to find in a good babysitter. Parents consider a babysitter an employee of their family; they will approach choosing a babysitter just as they would when finding an employee at their job. Babysitting is a very important job. Most parents will spend a good amount of time finding the best babysitter they can, so you need to be the best. You will be caring for children, and what is more meaningful than that? A good babysitter will need to meet certain criteria in order to find a job, and to accomplish that job expertly.

Most parents search for common attributes among babysitters. The list below explains many of the traits that parents consider. You need to make a great impression on parents and you need to have, or be willing to develop, these qualities in order to be a good babysitter.

These are some of the most common traits that parents look for in babysitters:

- **Dependability and responsibility**
  These two traits go hand in hand. If you can be trusted to show up on time, take care of the children's health and safety, not forget jobs, and be prepared for jobs then you are on the right track to becoming a great babysitter.

- **Enjoy spending time with children**
  If you like the children you are babysitting and children in general, then the experience of babysitting will be much more enjoyable for both you and the children. Also, kids seem to know if you like them or not by the way you act towards them. If you don't like children, then babysitting probably is not for you.

- **Adaptability**
  You must be able to react quickly and easily to change. When you are babysitting every house will be unique and there will be different rules and traditions. You need to be able to adapt easily to these differences and respect these differences. Also, you can never be prepared for everything, don't let surprises throw you off balance. You will need to flow easily with changes and situations that you may not have anticipated.

- **Maturity**
  You need to be levelheaded and act calmly when babysitting. You will have to deal with parents, children and make adult decisions, so you need to act like an adult. Taking care of someone else's children and home is a huge responsibility. Maturity is a must.

- **Safety consciousness**
  You need to protect the children, the house, and yourself against harm. Be aware of your surroundings at all times and make sure the kids and you are always safe. You must be able to anticipate or see a possibly unsafe situation before it happens. You can never be too safe.

- **Self-confidence**
  You must be sure of yourself when you make decisions. Before you carryout any decisions you must think about any potential consequences of your actions and decisions. It helps to write down the possible pros and cons of any decision before you act on it.

- **Demonstrate good manners**

  This is crucial if you want to get more and more babysitting jobs. You need to respect the house, children, parents, friends, neighbors, pets, and any other aspects of the job. Having good manners never hurts, and no one likes rude people. You can also teach the youngsters you are babysitting proper manners through your good example. The famous entertainer Fred Astaire said it best when he was quoted saying "the hardest job kids face today is learning good manners without seeing any."

- **Knowledgeable about children**

  You will want to know something about children if you want to babysit. Take time to learn about kids. Reading this book is a good step. As you babysit more and more you will learn about children.

- **Maintain a good reputation**

  You need to be known as someone who is kind and an all around good person in order to secure babysitting jobs. No one wants a bully or mean person watching his or her children. Act pleasantly and courteously toward all people even when you are not babysitting.

These nine attributes are what most parents strive for in a babysitter. If you meet them all great, you have a marvelous start to becoming a wonderful babysitter. If you don't quite meet them all, don't worry. It takes practice to become good at anything. With hard work and determination you can prove to every parent that you are the best babysitter for his or her children.

When parents search for a babysitter they do not just consider the nine personality attributes listed above. Yes, these attributes are quite important but they are not the only considerations. Here is a list of items that are also crucial to parents as they choose a babysitter.

- **Availability**
  You must be available to work when the family needs you. You may be the best-qualified babysitter in the entire universe, but if you are too busy to babysit then you will not find many jobs. You must communicate clearly to parents when you can and can not work. Inform them if you can work weekends, on holidays (remember not all families celebrate the same holidays), after school, on school nights and tell them how late you can babysit. If you are involved in too many activities you may need to stop some of them to free up more time for babysitting if that is what you really want to do. The more time you are available to babysit then chances are you will get more jobs.

- **Proximity to the family**
  If you live close to the families who you are babysitting or have reliable transportation to and from their homes, chances are you will be asked to babysit for them more often. Some different forms of transportation that many babysitters utilize are cars (your own, your parents or the people you are babysitting for), buses, trains, bikes, and even your own two feet. It is always easier to live close to someone when you are babysitting. Most parents prefer that you have your own transportation to and from their house. If you do, then you will be that much more likely to get the job. If you are an exemplary babysitter some parents will be willing to drive to your house to pick you up and to drive you home when you have completed.

- **Skills you possess**
  Parents also evaluate your skills when they are attempting to find a babysitter. Can you cook or prepare snacks and lunch food? Can you help the kids with homework? Can you do light cleaning if you and the children happen to create a mess? Can you change diapers and give a child a bath? These are all skills that parents search for in a babysitter. If you do not already have these skills you soon will because this book will teach all of them to you.

- **Affiliations**

  Many parents when deciding if they want you for a babysitter, will look at other activities or groups in which you belong. If you are a Girl Scout or Boy Scout, for example, chances are you will have many of the traits needed to be a great babysitter because these organizations build character and teach you skills. Also belonging to church organizations, YWCA, YMCA, school clubs, and other activities demonstrate to the parents that you are an outstanding member of the community. Prove to parents everywhere through your actions and activities that you are the best babysitter for them.

- **Pay**

  Some parents may choose a babysitter who charges less for their babysitting services. If a parent asks you how much you charge for babysitting do not be stuck on a certain amount. Tell them that you take whatever is fair. If you don't have any idea what a fair amount to be paid is, ask your friends who babysit what they get paid. Your pay should be equitable to your friends. Once you go to a job for the first time and you find out that the pay is not as much as you would have hoped, you then have a few options. One option is that you can ask for more money. If you did a great job the first time then the parents might be willing to pay you a bit more the next time. Most parents do not want to lose a great babysitter no matter what the cost. If this does not work you could always work for less money. Some families can't afford extra things in life. If you enjoy the kids and the family, you may consider working for less money. The experience of babysitting is invaluable itself and the family may recommend you to some other family who will pay more. Also some parents do not know what a fair price is to pay their babysitters. They may be new parents and the price that babysitters get compensated has gone up dramatically since they last babysat when they were your age. Don't worry about pay. You should focus on doing a great job when you babysit.

- **Boys vs. Girls**

  Traditionally girls have been recognized more as babysitters than boys. Girls are viewed as more motherly, more likely to enjoy children. These stereotypes are not true. Boys and girls are equally qualified when it comes to babysitting. A boy can be just as good a babysitter as a girl. Regardless if you are a boy or a girl, you should develop the skills needed to be a great babysitter. Don't be discouraged if you are a boy who wants to babysit and don't be over confident if you are a girl. Most parents will choose their babysitter on who can do the best job and who is the most qualified, not if they are a boy or a girl.

These skills and other factors are all important to parents who are looking for babysitters. But, when you are trying to find babysitting jobs you may be only one of many babysitters that the parents are considering. To have yourself stand out even more you need to make a list of references, a resume, and learn to sell your skills.

The references and resume go hand in hand. A reference is a person who will recommend you to the parents who are looking for a babysitter as a great choice for a babysitter. In your reference list you should include your parents, any neighbors with whom you are close, previous people who you have babysat for and any other people who will give you a positive recommendation. You will want to put the person's name, the relationship (neighbor, for example) and their phone number or other contact information. When you choose your four or five references, you will need to ask the people for permission first and only pick people who you think will give you a positive recommendation. The reference list should be given to the parents who may be considering you for a babysitting job.

Here is an example of what your reference list may look like. Your contact information should go first followed by your references name, relation to you, and phone number.

Sammy Sitter
100 Playtime Way
Funtown, USA
555-0132
SafeSammy@greatsitter.com

References

Mr. And Mrs. Sitter – parents,
Phone - 555-0132

Mr. And Mrs. Johnson - I babysit for their two
children,
Phone - 555-0929

Nurse Confidence-Sunny Day Hospital where I
volunteer,
Phone - 555-9291

Mr. Peters – history teacher at Valley View
Junior High,
Phone - 555-8623

A resume is similar to a reference list but instead of putting down people's names and numbers you will list any other places that you may have worked, any groups or organizations you belong to, and any awards or accomplishments that you have earned. A resume allows people to see who you are and what you have accomplished. A resume should not be more than one side of a piece of paper. If you have any other questions about resumes and reference lists, ask your parents. If they have ever been in the working world then they will know all about them.

Here is an example of what your resume may look like.

Sammy Sitter
100 Playtime Way
Funtown, USA
555-0132
SafeSammy@greatsitter.com

Experience

- I volunteer at Sunny Day Hospital where I play with hospitalized children.

- I have been babysitting for the Johnson family for six months. They have a two-year-old and a six-year-old.

Skills

I am very organized, punctual and responsible. I have also taken a first aid class in school and I am a member of the chess club.

Once you have learned all the above skills you next need to learn how to sell them to the parents of kids who will be hiring you. To learn to sell your skills construct a list of questions that the parents may ask you and then write down a good answer that you would be likely to give. This way you can anticipate any questions that may be asked of you. You may want to use the Babysitting Journal section of this book to write down your questions and answers. The Babysitting Journal is located at the end of this book.

Some questions that parents may ask you are:

-How long have you been babysitting?

-What skills do you have?

-What other activities do you participate?

-Do you like kids?

-When are you available to babysit?

-What do you charge?

These are a few examples of questions that parents may ask you. Write down your answers and try to remember what they are. This way you will be ready to impress any parent who may ask you any question. You do not need to be nervous when you talk to parents. Answer their questions the best you can, smile, and attempt to keep constant eye contact. If they ask you a question you did not anticipate, think about it for a few seconds and then give an honest answer. If you do these things it will be obvious to the parents that you are mature, organized and a great choice as a babysitter.

Now you know what parent's desire in a babysitter. Since babysitting is a very significant job you will need to be prepared to do it well. Follow the above recommendations and you will be on your way to be a great babysitter.

Chapter Three

Am I Ready To Babysit?

The question of when to start babysitting really depends on one simple principle—when **YOU** are ready. Everyone matures at different speeds. If your friend's babysit and you don't feel you are quite ready, then wait until you feel comfortable. Some people may be ready to babysit when they are in junior high school while others may not be ready until they are in college or even after college. I recommend that the youngest grade that someone starts to babysit should be around the sixth or seventh grade. However, everyone matures differently and some people may be ready to babysit earlier than this. At one of my babysitting jobs, for example, I was babysitting for a kid older than I was. I was thirteen at the time and was babysitting for someone who was fourteen. I was very mature and responsible for my age, so age does not often matter. What matters is how prepared you are to take care of other people's children.

Some communities do have laws and regulations regarding how old someone can be before they babysit. In Prince William County Virginia, for example the Department of Social Services suggests that a babysitter between the ages of twelve to thirteen only babysit children up to four hours. If you are fourteen through fifteen you may babysit over four hours, but not overnight. And they suggest that if you are sixteen and older you may babysit overnight. There are similar regulations and guidelines for babysitting in communities across the country.

Before you jump into babysitting there are a few things that must be understood. The children that you will be babysitting could be friends for life. You will see them grow up. You will see them and their parents around town. You must understand and be willing to take on the responsibility and consequences of your first job. You need to be willing to accept the fact that these youngsters will admire you and expect you to treat them as a friend. If you do a poor job babysitting it may be impossible for you to find another job because parents talk to other parents about their babysitters. Babysitting is not a job such as working in a store where once the store closes your job stops. Babysitting is job that creates bonds and friends for life, be certain you do it correctly.

One great way to find out if you are ready to babysit is to determine your goals. Ask yourself, what do I want to get out of this experience?

Here are a few goals you may want to keep in mind when deciding if you would like to become a babysitter.

- **Money**
  Money is a goal that is obvious for babysitting or any job. However, you should have a goal focusing on the monetary result. You could save it for going out with your friends, save it for school, or start saving to buy a car or something else in the future. But don't allow money be your only focus.

- **Expanding your skills**
  Expanding your skills is an enriching goal of babysitting. Babysitting teaches you how to be responsible, how to take care of a house, how to take care of yourself and most importantly, how to take care of children. The skills you learn while babysitting are very influential for later in your life. You may consider adding your babysitting jobs as references for other jobs or even on college applications. Who knows, maybe one of the parents you babysit for will offer you a job at the company where they work when you get older.

- **Learning about children**
  Learning about children is a very logical goal in babysitting. You may have children of your own someday. Babysitting will allow you to learn more about children so when you do have these tiny bundles of joy you will be more experienced in dealing with them.

- **Meeting new people**
  Meeting and becoming friends with new people is always enjoyable. While babysitting you might get to know your neighbors, family friends and other people who you might not have ever known. The more people you meet the more potential babysitting jobs and friends you will enjoy.

- **Learning about more cultures**
  Babysitting will give you the opportunity to meet all sorts of people and to be involved in all sorts of cultures and families. You may get the opportunity to eat different foods, learn about different holidays and other rituals of cultures other than your own. Who knows, you may even learn a new language or at least a few words in a new language other than your own. With the changing demographics in America today you will almost certainly have the opportunity to meet people from other countries and cultures while babysitting. In 2001 it is estimated that nineteen percent of all children living in the United States have at least on parent who is born in a foreign country.

- **Having fun**
  Babysitting is one of the only jobs in the world where you can earn money and play at the same time. You learn about games that are popular with children and you might find that the kids you are babysitting play some of the same games that you and your friends enjoy or played when you were younger. Babysitting, at times, can be more fun than work.

- **Social skills**

  Babysitting will help you develop great social skills. You will need to learn how to interact with children and adults while babysitting. This interaction gives you the confidence needed to be a well-developed adult. You will learn how to ask questions, think rationally, and quickly. Babysitting will make you more mature and comfortable in social situations.

If you are not really sure what your goals are, that is also okay. If you want to see if you like bike riding, you learn how to ride a bike. This works for babysitting as well. If you want to see if you might like it, try it.

If you are still not sure if babysitting is for you, ask someone you know who does it. See if your peers babysit. Talk to older siblings or the older siblings of your friends about their experiences while babysitting. Maybe you could join one of your friends when they are babysitting as a helper. If you would like to do this ask your friend and ask the parents of the children that they will be babysitting. This will allow you to see what a real babysitting job is like.

Another great way to learn about kids without having to actually babysit is by being a mother's helper. This is when you work at a home watching children while the parent is home. The parent may work at home or be doing other activities that do not allow them to give all of their attention to their children. This type of work may not pay as well as actual babysitting, but it is great experience and will teach you about children without having the responsibility of being entirely alone with the kids.

If you still aren't sure about babysitting then try it on your younger siblings or relatives first. If you don't or can't babysit for younger siblings, then try to take care of an animal. This might sound rather silly, but give it a whirl. Consider taking care of a puppy. If you feed it, clean it and walk it for a while and it is happy and healthy then you have proven to yourself that you are responsible. Yes, children are different than a puppy, but they are also rather similar, they all need you to take care of them.

Once you decide to babysit but are not quite convinced that it is for you, start out slowly. Babysit for only a few hours at a time at first and gradually add more hours. Try to find people who only need someone to babysit their children for a couple of hours. This will really let you see if babysitting is for you. If you enjoy babysitting for a few hours, then you may be ready for longer hours and more families to babysit.

Below are a few questions to ask yourself to gauge if you are ready to babysit.

- Am I responsible?
- Do I want to earn some money?
- Do I like children?
- Do children like me?
- Am I flexible with my schedule?
- Will babysitting help me reach my goals?
- Can I stay out late at night babysitting if I need to?
- Do I follow directions well?
- Do I know, or can learn, first aid?
- Am I willing to learn new things?

If you answered "yes" to most of these questions, then you may be ready to babysit.

Chapter Four

How To Start Babysitting

Once you have decided that you would like to babysit, you need to locate families and kids to babysit. This can be very difficult or very easy depending on how you approach getting your first job. As you start searching for babysitting jobs keep track of everything you do, people you talk to, and places you go, to see what works the best in finding jobs. This information could be helpful to you later.

To keep track of all this information you need to be organized. The first thing you will need is this book. Use the back of this book to write down the names of the people you talk to, their phone numbers and when they want you to babysit for them. You will also need a copy of your resume and reference list, which are both discussed in chapter two as well as a list of your skills.

As you go about finding babysitting jobs do not become discouraged, there are plenty of kids out there that need a great babysitter like you. In the year 2000 it was estimated that there were seventy and a half million children in this country. And by the year 2020 it is projected that twenty four percent of the population of the United States will be children. There is definitely not a lack of children in this country and all of them need to have a great babysitter.

Follow the steps below in order to find people who need a babysitter.

- **Talk to friends**
  Your first step should be to ask your friends if they babysit. If they do, ask if you might be able to do it for them if they can't one day or

night. This will give you some experience and a real feel for what babysitting is all about without feeling obligated to babysit long term.

However, this approach might also cause some conflict with you and your friends if you are a better babysitter than they are. If you are, then you may get your friend's job permanently!

- **Ask your parents**
  Another way to get clients is to ask your parents if they know anyone who needs a babysitter. This is a good way to get your first job with someone who your parents know and that you might feel comfortable with.

- **Design Business Cards**
  You can make business cards with your name, phone number or e-mail address on them. These could be simple or very elaborate with colors and creative fonts. Once you create your cards, pass them out to friend's parents and your neighbors with youngsters. However, before you pass out any cards make sure your parents go with you when you visit your neighbors. It is always best to be safe, and you don't want just anyone having your name and phone number.

Here is an example of a business card. Most business cards are small and can fit easily in your pockets.

NEED A BABYSITTER?

Hire Sammy Sitter

call me at 555-0132
or e-mail me at SafeSammy@greatsitter.com

Refrences available upon request

- **Visit your School Counselor**
  You can visit your school counseling center or office and ask if there is a job board where you can post one of your cards, or possibly find people who are attempting to locate babysitters in the area. Again, you will want to be sure you are being safe when you let other people have your name and phone number.

- **Local Papers**
  You can glance through your community or church newspaper for listings of people needing babysitters. Sometimes people who need a babysitter will post an ad.

- **Post an Ad**
  You can post an ad in a local or church newspaper offering your babysitting skills. Placing an ad may cost a few dollars, but it will pay off in the long run once you start to get jobs.

- **Design Flyers**
  A flyer is a piece of paper which advertises something. People make flyers to advertise yard sales, help wanted, lost animals and a variety of other items. You can make flyers selling your babysitting skills. When you design a flyer you will want to be sure your target audience knows who you are, what skills you possess and how to get a hold of you. You may want to hand out your flyers to neighbors with children, at day care centers and other locations where parents with young children tend to congregate.

If these approaches don't work right away, remain patient and always keep your ears and eyes open. You never know when and where you might find a family who needs a good babysitter. Also, there are other ways to find babysitting jobs that may give you experience and maybe some pay. To follow is a list of places where you can get some experience and possibly find some babysitting jobs. Then we will explore places where you may get paid and also find babysitting jobs. All of the places listed below can be added to your resume and some of the people you meet may be added to your list of references.

Places where you can get more experience and perhaps more jobs:

- **Volunteer at a hospital**
  Most hospitals have a pediatric unit, which is a department in the hospital that takes care of kids. In these units there may be an area where you can volunteer to play with some of the hospitalized children. Some hospitals also have programs where you take care of one child for the entire afternoon. You may take walks with them, play games, and just talk with them. Volunteering in a hospital will be a great experience. You will learn how to deal with children, and you may even pick up some first aid techniques, which are always helpful in babysitting. Who knows, you may even find your future career as a doctor, nurse, or physical therapist while volunteering in a hospital.

- **Volunteer at your local library**
  Many libraries have programs where people from the community read stories to children. You could be the volunteer to read the stories or help supervise the kids. Doing this will teach you more about children. You will learn how to interact with children, learn about the latest children's books and you will meet many parents who can potentially hire you to babysit.

- **Volunteer to work at birthday parties**
  You can get more experience with kids by working at neighborhood birthday parties. These could be parties that your younger siblings have or the parties of neighborhood kids that you may know. While attending these parties you can observe how kids play and what the latest games are that kids enjoy. You will also meet other parents who may need a babysitter just like you!

- **Volunteer at a church**
  Many churches have either day cares or a time for children to go to Sunday School while their parents are at the service. If your church does have a program like this, you could volunteer your time and skills to help the teachers with the children. This will give you some of the skills needed to deal with children as well as meeting other parents who may want to hire you as their babysitter.

- **Take a class about babysitting**
  Many YMCA's, YWCA's and local community centers have classes that will teach you how to be a better babysitter. These classes will most likely go over some of the ideas and skills that this book teaches you. Check with your local community center and see if they have a class for you.

Now we are going to go over places where you can get more experience, earn some money and maybe get more babysitting jobs.

- **Work for a licensed daycare**
  A great place to learn more childcare skills and to earn some extra money is by working for a daycare. There are many different types of daycares and it is estimated that there are 113,298 regulated childcare centers in the United States. Some require that you have a license from the state in which you live in order to work there, but you may be able to get a job at a daycare as a part time helper. If you do get a job at a daycare you will learn a great deal about children and will meet many parents who may need your babysitting skills.

- **Work for a summer or sports camp**
  Working for camps is a great way to learn about kids, meet parents and make a little money. There are many different types of camps. There are some camps that are for sports, some for daytime care, some for church groups and some for all around merriment. You

can learn about various camps by visiting your town's city hall or recreation department.

You can learn many valuable skills working for a camp, but depending on what type of camp will dictate what type of skills you will learn. If you work at a sports camp, for example, then you will most likely learn new games, how to teach kids games, how to play fairly and how to organize a large group of children. If you work at a general summer camp you may learn new arts and crafts, new songs and meet numerous youngsters with a variety of interests.

You now have some good ideas about how to meet parents and hopefully get some babysitting jobs. It may take a little while for you to find people to babysit, but once you do then more and more jobs will most definitely follow. Once you start getting calls for jobs, write down who the person is, where they heard about you, and any other information you may need. Also you don't want to schedule more than one babysitting job on the same day at the same time. That will make you appear unorganized and foolish. Stay organized. As you get more and more jobs you will find out that the best way to expand your business is by word of mouth. This happens when the people who you babysit tell their friends about you and then their friends ask you to babysit for their kids. The more you work and the better job you do, the more jobs you will get.

Also, keep in mind that your number one goal when you search for babysitting jobs is YOUR SAFETY. Always ensure a parent is with you when you visit with strangers. It is always better to be safe than sorry. If you don't feel comfortable for any reason with a job offer, you do not need to take it.

Chapter Five

Starting Your First Job...And How To Keep It

Once you find a family who wants you to babysit for them you will need to find out a few crucial bits of information. It is paramount to learn these things once you have accepted the job, the first time that you talk to them. This could be either in person, on the telephone or by e-mail.

You need to find out...

—how many kids they have
—how old is each child
—what are their names
—detailed directions to their house
—their phone number
—what hours they need you
—what day they need you
—how you will get to their house (will you drive, will they pick you up or will you get there some other way)
—how they found your name and number
—if they have any questions for you

You will want to repeat back all the information to the parents. This way there will not be any misunderstanding about anything. You also want to speak clearly and make a great first impression. If you are courteous and clear on the phone then the parents of the kids that you will be babysitting will think positively of you even before you meet face to face.

It also helps to write the kids' names and ages on a piece of paper that you keep in your pocket until you can remember their names. If you know the kids' names the first time you meet them, then they will respect you more and your first babysitting experience will be more positive than if you forget their names or call them by the wrong name.

It is also a good idea to meet the parents and children before you first babysit for them. You could arrive early the first day of your first job to meet the kids and parents to go over the rules. When you first meet the parents and kids it is also a good idea to have one of your parents with you if any questions or concerns arise.

- **The most important thing that you can do at your first job is follow the rules.**

Each family will have different or varying rules that you must follow. If you follow the rules then your chances of being asked back to babysit greatly increase.

Also, when you babysit you should have a babysitting bag. It is a bag or backpack that you will carry with you on all babysitting jobs that contains certain items that you may need. Following are some items that you should keep in your babysitting bag.

Items for your babysitting bag:

- First aid items such as bandages and sanitary wipes. These are always useful if you or one of the kids get a small cut or scrape.
- A watch so you always know the time.
- This book to answer any questions that you have and to help you if you need it.
- A toy that you don't mind giving to the child. This toy can be used as an icebreaker to play with a child when you first meet him or her.

If you show the child that you are fun, then there is a better chance that he or she will like you.

- Several children's books and coloring books.
- A deck of cards.
- Any phone numbers that you need. This includes your number, and the number of the people that you are babysitting.
- Your identification. This can be a school ID, a driver's license, or any other paper that will let people know who you are.
- Some extra money just in case you need to buy something while you are babysitting.
- A small flashlight just in case the power goes out or you need to light up a dark area.
- A pen or pencil.

As you do more and more babysitting you may want to add a few items or remove some. It is always better to be overly prepared than not prepared enough. Some other items that you could include in your babysitting bag are a hat, sunglasses, a granola bar or other food just in case you or the kids get hungry and are not near food, sunscreen and a cell phone. A cell phone is not needed in most cases, but if the parents let you use one of their phones for emergencies that would be great.

We are now going to go over the steps that you should take when you go to a job for the first time.

- When you meet the parents and kids be very courteous. Strive to get their names correct and smile. A simple smile tells a child that you are a kind person and they will be more likely to like you.

- Go over the rules and the house with the parents. Have them point out any hazards such as electrical outlets, steep stairways, or other things that may harm you or the children. Also have them point out any safety items such as smoke detectors, fire extinguishers and escape ladders in case of fire. Walk through the house with the parents as they go over the rules.

- Find out about the children's babysitting history. Have they been left with a babysitter before? What are their reactions to being left alone? Do the children have any physical or mental conditions you need to know about? Try to get to know the children and family as best you can.

- Ask the parents if you need to give the youngsters a bath, feed them or put diapers on any of them. Make sure you know where the food is, what they need for a bath, and what diapers to use when changing a child.

- Find out if the children are allowed to play outside. If they are, what are their restrictions?

- Ask the parents if the children need to take any medications. Also, ask them if the children are allergic to any foods or medications.

- Go over what areas of the house are for playing and find out what bedrooms the children should go into at bedtime.

- Find out where the parents are going. Get the phone number of where you can reach them if you need to plus their cell phone number if they have one. Find out when they will return home.

- Be sure you get any important phone numbers from the parents. These numbers could include the place they are going, the neighbor's number, the fire and police department's numbers, the pediatrician's number or any other phone numbers that you may need.

- Find out what the kids can play with and if they are allowed to watch television or movies. If they are, then find out what the kids can watch. You don't want to have a child watching something that their parents do not approve.

- Find out when bedtime is and ask if the children need to take naps. If they do ask what time and how long the naps should be.

- Ask the parents what type of discipline you should use if their children get out of hand. Some sample disciplines are timeout, taking a toy from a child, or putting them to bed. The question of discipline is a very touchy subject. You NEVER want to hit, push, or pull a child. If the kids get unmanageable, call their parents.

- If there are any family pets find out if they can go outside, need to be fed or any other special things about the pets.

- Make sure that you understand and remember all the house rules. If you don't, have the parents write them down or you can write them down yourself.

Yes, this is a long list of items that you need to remember. However, they are all significant. As you babysit more and more, getting this information from the parents will come easier for you. Always remember the more questions you have the better, even if they may seem silly. If you are not clear on a rule or what you should do in a certain situation, just ask.

If you do not follow a rule, chances are the kids will tell their parents. Kids tend to tell their parents everything that you do, what you played and what you ate. So if you break the rules, then you might lose your job. Kids also test babysitters from time to time. They will tell you the opposite of what their parents told you just to see what you do. Don't be fooled by the kids. Always do what their parents say and use your best judgement.

It is better to prepare for anything than to be surprised by everything.

We are now going to go through a sample babysitting job. However, every babysitting job will be different. This example is only to show you the general structure of what a job that you have may be like. In this example the job takes place in the evening.

- First, you need to show up on time or a little bit early. This is your chance to make a great first impression. Make sure you greet the parents and meet the kids. Try to know the kids' names if possible.

- Then you will go through the house and over any lists or rules that the parents have for you. This is your time to ask any questions or address any concerns that you have. Find out where the parents are going and about when they will be back.

- Once the parents leave it is time to play some games with the kids. If it is still light outside and warm, you may want to play some outside games. If it is dark or colder it would be better to stay inside and play. This is the time that you will want to play your more active games. The kids may be feeling unhappy because their parents left, so you need to keep them active and tire them out.

- Once they have played for a while it will be time to feed the children. You may need to feed them dinner or just a snack. Make sure you have found out what they can and can not eat from their parents before they leave. Once dinner is over you and the kids need to clean up the food and dishes. Attempt to leave the house cleaner than the way you found it. This is very important because parents enjoy arriving home to a neat, tidy and clean home.

- After dinner you can again play some games. This time, however, you should play quiet games. The kids will have full tummies so you do not want them to do anything overly active. Also, since it is getting closer to bedtime you do not want to get the kids running around. If they get overly active then it will be very difficult to get them to sleep. Also, if the kids need to do homework or practice an instrument or do some other activity, this would be the time.

- After they are finished playing or doing homework you might want to let the kids have a snack or get some dessert. This is also a good time to begin to discuss bedtime with the children. Tell them how long it is until bedtime and what they need to do before bedtime.

- Once their dessert is over it is time for the kids to wind down. You can read them a book, watch a movie or the TV quietly or play a calm game. This is a time for you and the kids to relax.

- Once all of you are relaxed it is time for them to get ready for bed. This can include getting a bath, brushing teeth, going to the bathroom, getting bottles and putting on their pajamas among other things. Getting the kids ready for bed can either be a breeze or can be very hectic. Keep the kids moving and don't let them stall too much.

- Once they are ready for bed and it is bedtime, get the kids into their appropriate beds and say good night. Chances are the kids will not go to bed easily. If they give you trouble, do your best and eventually they will fall asleep. It is paramount that you let the kids know where you will be if they need anything. Also be certain the night-lights they are accustomed to are on and the room is how they like it.

- Once the kids are in bed it is your time to do what you want. You could watch TV quietly or read a book. You should not do anything noisy and you should always be in a place where you can hear the kids just in case they get up or begin to fuss. You should peek in on the sleeping children to be certain that they are asleep. You should check them about every thirty minutes to ensure they are fine. Just because the kids are in bed does not mean that your job is over, or that they are asleep.

- Once the parents come home you should give them a brief summary of the evening. Tell them what went right and what went wrong. Do not attempt to hide anything and do tell them anything that you think they may need to know. It is also at this time that you should be paid for your babysitting services. You might also discuss the next time that the parents want you to babysit. Say good night and you are finished.

This is just an example of what you could expect at an evening babysitting job. It is important to keep the kids busy and do a variety of activities. You don't want to do the same things all evening long.

If you follow these steps and rules listed in this chapter then you should be ready to start your first babysitting job. The most crucial thing to remember is that a great first impression is extremely important. You need to come across as a responsible person who will do their best. Also, be sure you are honest with the parents. If something goes wrong let them know. Surprisingly enough the more honest you are (even if what you tell them is not good news) chances are you will still be asked back to babysit again and again. Honesty is imperative.

Chapter Six

Having Fun On The Job

Babysitting is one of the only jobs in the world where you get paid to act like a kid. I know that it might not always be cool to play with younger kids or their toys, but as you start to play with kid's toys you may find that you are having more fun than the kids are. Be goofy, make silly faces, paint pictures and play with trains. This is your chance to act like a kid again, so enjoy it.

When you meet a child for the first time on a new babysitting job it is important that you play with them before their parents leave. This is especially important when dealing with younger children. If you immediately play with the little ones this will tell them that you are okay. It will also cut down on the possibility of the child becoming hysterical when their parents do leave, which may happen from time to time. Playing with a youngster when the parents are still there also demonstrates to the parents that you are indeed a great babysitter because you take an immediate interest in their child.

The way to start playing with a child is to observe what they were doing when you came to the door. If, for example, they have a doll or truck in their hands then help them play with that toy. You may also want to bring a toy with you that can be used to play with the child when you first arrive. This could be the toy that you keep in your babysitter's bag. However, I do suggest that you do not bring a toy that means something special to you because it may get lost or broken.

Most of your time babysitting should be spent playing with the children. You are there to care for them, and entertaining them is a large part of caring for them. When you play games with the children, keep them busy. Play games that are active, games that challenge them to think, and games that are most importantly FUN. If the kids are not having fun then chances are you, too, will not be having a good time.

When you start to play with the children who you are babysitting you need to find out where their toys are located. This might not seem as easy a task as you might imagine. There could be toys in the child's room, in a playroom, in closets or in the basement. When you see where the toys are located make a mental note as to what toys there are so if a child gets bored you can suggest another toy that you know they have. This brings up another point. Never ask the child if they have a certain toy, especially if it is the latest, most popular toy. If you do ask this question and they do not have the toy but want it, they may become sad or angry. You don't want to have to deal with a sad or angry kid because of a toy. However, if a child shows you a favorite toy of theirs, give the toy a positive comment. If they have a favorite doll that has bright red hair, for example, comment on how you like the doll's hair. Also, ask the child questions about their toys. Ask them, for example, what the doll's name is, how old their truck is or what color the action figure's hat is. The child will like the fact that you have taken an interest in their toys.

If there are disagreements over a particular toy that more than one child wants to play with at a time, the best thing that you can do is first put forth an effort to distract the fighting children. Divert their attention away from the problematic toy onto other toys or activities. You can do this by suggesting you all play a different game or activity. If the kids are fighting over a truck, start playing with a puzzle.

If this does not work then you can physically take the problematic toy away from the kids. When you do this take the toy and put it out of the kid's sight. They will more than likely not like this so immediately give suggestions about other toys they can play with. The sooner you get their minds off the problematic toy, the better. This may cause more problems because the children may start fighting with you as well as fighting with each other.

A third action that you could take is set a time limit on the popular toy. Allow one child to play with the toy for five minutes and then allow the other child to play with the toy for five minutes. This way they both get to play with the toy and will hopefully both be content. You will discover that most kid's attention span for one toy is so short that they will probably not play with any one toy for more than a few minutes.

Also, you never know what a youngster may use for a toy. Simple items such as coaster or a blanket may be used for hours of playtime enjoyment. Children tend to take normal items and turn them into toys. They may make up games and stories with the items. If the items will not hurt the kid and they are safe to play with then let the child play with them. Just because an object is not sold as a toy does not mean that it can not be used as a toy.

When you play games with children there will almost always need to be a winner. This can cause some problems if you are not careful, especially if they are playing against you. Try to allow the children to win a few games, but the key is not to let them know that you are letting them win. If you are playing a board game, for example, and it is obvious that you are not trying your best, kids will feel cheated that you do not think they are good enough at the game. You need to be sneaky when you lose. Also, you don't have to lose all the time in every game that you play. Never take a game seriously. You need to exemplify good sportsmanship. Teach the youngsters fairness and don't allow anyone to cheat or harm another player. The children learn from your example, so make it a good one.

Games are exciting for both you and the kids you are babysitting, but never forget that you are still working and caring for children. Do these entertaining activities when it is the proper time and always be aware what you are doing and what the kids are doing at all times. Never forget the safety and well being of the children come first no matter how good a time you may be having.

Playing games and keeping the kids occupied will make the time go much faster, and will make it more enjoyable for all. The best way to do this is by playing active games. Games where you and the kids get some physical activity and enjoyment. Sure you could watch television the whole time, but that will not be very entertaining, so play games.

However, before you dive right into playtime, you need to think about safety. Follow these rules for safe inside and outside activities.

Inside Safety

- Keep floors and play areas clean. It is important that all areas that you or the child will be walking in are clean. You don't want to step on something that could cut your feet or cause you to slip and fall.

- Play in a designated area that the parents tell you about. Be sure you and the children know where you can and can not play. A safe play area should not be near stairs, have any uncovered power outlets nearby or be near any open windows or doors which the child could run away or fall out.

- Remove toys and objects that may be dangerous to children. These could be items that have pointy edges and other hazards that may cut, scrape, or fall on children such as heavy things on tables that a child could pull onto themselves. Also keep all cords and rope away from kids. If there are any cords on the blinds or drapes ensure they are tucked away out of the children's reach. A child can easily get entangled in a cord and choke to death.

- Check stuffed animals and other toys for buttons and small parts that may be loose or falling off. Children can easily swallow these tiny items.

- Get the youngsters in the habit of putting away toys before they get out new ones. This will cut down on the clutter and the possibility of getting hurt by a toy that may be lying around.

- Make sure the toys that the children are playing with are for their age. Most toys are geared towards certain age groups and if a younger child plays with a toy intended for an older child, there may be parts on the toy that could harm him or her.

- Keep toys within reach of a child when they are playing with them. This will keep the child in the safe area and will ensure that nothing dangerous happens.

- Don't let the kids throw toys around the room. This can be dangerous to you, the child, and the room. Also, be especially watchful when the kids are playing with battery operated toys. These types of toys may contain small batteries that the kids can choke on and may also be fire hazards.

- Always keep an eye on the kids when they are playing. If there are rooms that are off limits, make sure that the kids and you stay out of these particular rooms.

Outside Safety

- Before you allow anyone to play outside, check the entire play area for any safety hazards. Be sure to inform the children about any out of bounds areas that are forbidden. Some safety hazards to look for are holes in the ground, sprinklers that are sticking up, prickly plants, snakes and other animals as well as pools, streets, bees and anything else that may potentially harm the children.

- Check out any play equipment such as jungle gyms or swing sets for anything that may harm the children. These could include rough edges on the equipment, dirty equipment, and any other hazards that you see. If it does not appear safe then don't play on it.

- Make sure any potentially dangerous animals or unleashed dogs are not in the area. Not all dogs and animals are friendly and some may have diseases and will bite.

- Be extremely cautious of swimming pools, spas, wading pools, and any other areas where water is present. Stay away from them at all times. You should not let the children go swimming when you babysit. It is too risky. Be sure that all gates are locked around pools and always be vigilant when anyone is near water. A child can drown in less than an inch of water.

- Designate a play area and let the children know the boundaries. Do not allow them to stray from that area. When you find a play area make sure it is an area that you can see the whole time. You don't want to have an area so large that you can not keep track of the kids.

- Try to keep a portable telephone with you if you play outside just in case you need to call for help. Also, make sure you have a key to the house or have some other way to get back in just in case you get locked out.

- Don't wander off or let the kids wander off. You must stay with the kids the entire time. If you see something that is out of the play area that interests you, ignore it. You need to focus on the children. There are potentially more hazards outside than inside so be alert. Some children are wanderers, so watch them at all times.

- Do not allow children to cross any street by themselves. When you do cross a street hold the child's hand or be sure they are in a stroller. Always use crosswalks and obey all traffic signals and laws. Always look both ways before you cross any street. It helps to look both ways a few times just to make sure you did not miss anything. Avoid crossing busy streets or crossing streets when it is dark.

- The bottom line for outside safety is to keep track of the kids at all times and keep them safe. If you feel uncomfortable having the kids outside for any reason, then take them back inside and play.

Now on with the games! Below is a list of games for oozers and for kids of all different ages for both inside and outside. These are just a few suggestions of games you might try. Remember you can always design your own games or play new games.

GAMES FOR OOZERS

When it comes to playing games with oozers you need to be a bit more creative than you do with older, more developed children. Children this age can not participate in as many active games as older children. Toddlers this age need to develop their motor skills such as touching their toes or moving their arms. There are a few games designed with these skills in mind. However, these games can still be fun for both you and the child. Here are a few ideas of games that you can play with oozers.

Play peek-a-boo with the youngster. This simple game seems to excite many oozers. When you play peek-a-boo most kids' eyes instantly light up as a big smile covers their face. You can also play with mirrors. Place the child in front of a mirror and let them view themselves. Children love to see their reflection. This can also keep a young child busy for a while, but be careful that they do not run into the mirror.

You can also roll balls to a child this age. Some may even be able to roll them back to you. Also, play blocks with the children. Simple blocks, like balls, can build hand eye coordination and are always fun to do. Other ideas are playing with puppets, rattles and making funny noises with your mouth. Kids this age seem to really enjoy it when they are talked to in baby talk, but don't talk baby talk to older kids because they need to learn how to speak in a normal manner.

When you play with oozers, keep them inside. Too much sun is damaging for young children's skin and the sun can harm their sensitive eyes. If you do go outside with them, make sure they are properly covered. Also, when you are playing with oozers put them on their back or have them sit up in a safe place. Always put them in an area where they can see you and you can see them. This will let them feel more comfortable and will also allow you to know where they are and what they are doing at all times. Also if there are other older kids in the family who you are babysitting, you may need to protect the oozers from them. Older children may attempt to pick up or poke the younger ones. Be careful when older, bigger kids are around smaller ones.

Oozers can be quite amusing. You can hold them in your arms and sing to them for hours. Just be gentle and give them undivided attention.

TOYS FOR ALL AGES

Most of your time playing will be spent playing with toys. Following is a list of different toys that are good for different ages of children. Also, most toys will have an age range on the toy itself or on the box. Look at these ranges and check to see if the child who you are babysitting is old enough to play with a particular toy.

- **Children under one year old**
  These kids enjoy bright colored toys that tend to be sturdy and washable. Since these children put everything in their mouths, their toys should be large enough so they can not swallow them. Rattles, washable stuffed animals, and dolls are all great toys for children this age.

- **Children one to two years old**
  Kids these ages are becoming more curious and are still putting their toys in their mouths. Some good toys for this age group are cloth blocks, books made out of stiff cardboard or cloth, and take-apart toys with large pieces.

- **Children two to three years old**
  These children are beginning to talk and are extremely curious about the world around them; their toys should reflect their growth. Toys two to three year olds might enjoy are wooden animals, wooden blocks, simple musical instruments, and large puzzles.

- **Children three to four years old**
  These kids are very imaginative and can be very physically active. Some entertaining toys for three to four year olds are sturdy trucks, musical instruments, simple board games, dolls, and large crayons.

- **Children four to six years old**
  These children are becoming more socially active as well as developing coordination and good hand eye skills. Some good toys for four to six year olds are blocks of different shapes and colors, picture books, felt boards, clay, paints, and cardboard games.

- **Children six to eight years old**
  These kids are very independent when they play. Some toys for six to eight year olds are kites, puppets, dolls, magnets, and reading books.

- **Children eight to ten years old**
  These kids are usually into science and arts and crafts. Possible toys for children these ages are construction sets or model sets, arts and craft kits, bikes, and other hobby materials.

These are just a few suggestions for children of all different ages. You will find that every child has a variety of toys and every child will enjoy unique preferences.

GAMES YOU CAN PLAY INSIDE

These games are all ones that should be played inside. Before you play any of these games you need to designate a safe area in which they will be played. If you are playing a board game, for example, create enough space for the board and any pieces that go along with it.

Sleeping Lions
(ages = all)
(for two or more children)

This game is very useful when the kids you are babysitting become a little rowdy and you want to calm them down. The point of this game is very simple. The kids strive to remain as quiet and motionless as possible. The first one to move is out. The winner of the game is the last person who does not move or make a sound. This will calm down kids and get them to compete with each other on who can be the quietest, which will make your job much easier. Be sure the participants play this game in a safe area where you can see them clearly.

Board Games
(ages = Three and up, depending on small pieces and ability)
(for one or more children)

Board games range in difficulty and types for different age groups and interests. Most families keep board games in a closet or other place. If they don't, you could bring one from your home and teach the kids how to play. Making up your own rules to traditional board games can be fun. This is especially useful if you or the kids do not know all the rules to a particular game, if some of the game pieces are missing or if the game is made for older people. Sometimes the children may surprise you concerning what kind of games they enjoy. For instance, on one of my babysitting jobs an eight-year-old taught me how to play chess. We played and he beat me over and over again, but I finally did learn how to play the game.

When playing board games leave your options open. Pick a game that is geared towards the kids you are babysitting. If you have kids that are different ages, pick a game geared toward the youngest child. Also, if the kids lose interest in a board game either start a new game, change the rules to make it more fun or do something entirely different.

Scavenger Hunt
(ages = Three and up, depending on their ability)
(for one or more children)

In a scavenger hunt you hide objects in the house, or ask the children to find particular items in the house. You go around the house and hide items such as stuffed animals, trucks, blocks and other toys and then have the kids find these items. You can design your scavenger hunt as simple or complex as you want, but always keep in mind the ages and ability of the kids that you are babysitting. You don't want to make the scavenger hunt too easy or too difficult.

You also might want to draw a map for the kids disclosing where you have hidden the items. This will transform your scavenger hunt into a treasure hunt. Always remember to not hide anything in a dangerous place or a place where the kids may get hurt. As the kids are searching for certain items always keep track of their location. Happy hunting!

Pretend
(ages = Three and up, depending on their ability)
(for one or more children)

Pretend is always enjoyable to do. The rules are simple; pretend to be something that you are not. Have the kids pretend they are their favorite animals, for example. Maybe you will all be monkeys or giant elephants. Utter the noises that these animals make and walk and talk to imitate them. You could also pretend to be a police officer or a teacher. If you are a police officer then you can pretend you are helping people. If you are a teacher you can have the children pretend they are teaching a lesson or grading papers. You could also take turns guessing what the other is pretending to be. Pretend is a great game to play if there are few other options available or if the kids have very active imaginations. The adventures and options in pretend are endless. Let your imagination run wild!

Put On A Play
(ages = all)
(for two or more children)

Most kids love to act. They love to act out the cartoons they see on TV and they may love to act like their favorite characters in movies and books. When you find a child who loves to act why don't you put on a play. Your play could either be very simple with just a few characters and a simple story; or a very fancy play with costumes (you could use old clothes or old sheets for costumes), a variety of characters and music. You can also have the children write their own plays. Take ideas from them and write them down for later. Then each of you will take a part and the show is on!

Once your play is complete the kids may want to perform it for their parents. If they do want to perform their play either do it before you next babysit for the family, after you babysit or decide on a time that fits your and the parent's schedule.

Put On A Concert
(ages = all)
(for one or more children)

Many children or you may play musical instruments. If so, why don't you put on a concert? Most kids will have either toy or real instruments in their house. Don't use real instruments without asking parental permission. If they do not have any instruments in their house this is not a problem. You can create instruments by simply taking a plastic bowl or cup and tap it lightly with a spoon or stick. You now have a drum. Many sturdy toys and other items can also become wonderful instruments. The bottom of an oatmeal container or bucket can make a fabulous drum and the cardboard roll in wrapping paper can make for a terrific flute or trumpet. Use your imagination when creating your own concert. It probably won't sound very good, but it will be entertaining. If you want to you could also record your concert on a tape player or computer if one is available.

- Always remember that you should not use any items that will break while putting on a concert. Use common sense when creating instruments. A glass bowl, for example, is not a good idea for a drum.

Hide And Seek
(ages = one and up, depending on the child)
(for three or more children)

The rules are simple for hide and seek. One person is "it" and the rest of the kid's hide. The person who is "it" counts to ten while the other kids hide somewhere in the house. Once the person who is "it" completes counting they will try to find the kids who are hiding. The first person they find will then be "it" and the game continues from there.

But before you count to ten and hide make sure you do a few things.

- First, lay down the rules. For instance, restrict certain parts of the house as off limits such as the kitchen, garage, or other places that can be potentially dangerous. Make sure everyone knows where are the off limit areas. Take a tour of the house and point out what areas are and are not for hiding. Create a rule that if anyone hides in an off limit area then he or she can not play the game and must sit quietly on the couch or in another designated safe area.

- Second, have a phrase or word such as "Game Over" be the key that everyone has to come out of hiding. This will ensure that no one stays hidden for a long while and that the game can move along smoothly to keep everyone's attention.

- Third, do your best to keep track of where the kids are hiding and let them have the enjoyment of you not guessing where they are each time. You should be "it" the first time or every time if the children like. Also if a young child does not comprehend the game, pair up with him and hide as a team.

Hide and seek is a great game to play with kids of all ages just as long as they can move fast enough to get away.

Card Games
(ages = Three and up, depending on their ability.)
(for two or more children)

Card games are also fairly common because most homes have a deck or two of cards and most kids enjoy playing with them. You can have the kids make up their own games with the cards or you could play traditional games such as Memory or Go Fish or even construct card castles by carefully stacking cards on top of each other.

Memory

Memory, or Concentration is a very common game for children. It is played using special cards that are made specifically for the game. Most Memory cards contain pictures of common objects such as a house, an elephant and other things on one side of the card. This is called the face side of the card. The other side of the card will be the same for all the cards. There will be two identical cards of each item. For example, there will be two cards of the same elephant, or two cards of the same house.

The rules are simple. You begin by placing all the cards face down, so you can not see the picture on the card. Spread the cards out so there are not any hidden cards. You will all take turns flipping over cards, trying to match them up with other cards that are the same. You can only turn over two cards on each turn that you have if you do not get a match. If the cards do not match, let's say you turn over a house and a car, then you must place the cards back where you found them face down and it is the next person's turn. If you do get a match, let's say you turn over two cards that both have a dog on them, then you can turn over another two cards until you do not get another match. You will keep the cards that match in your own separate pile. The person with the most matches once the game is over wins.

As you play Memory try to remember what cards are where. If you pick a certain card you may know where its match is. Memory is a fun and challenging game that can be played over and over again.

Go Fish

Go fish is played differently than Memory but you can use the same Memory cards when you play Go Fish. The point of Go Fish is to collect the most matching cards, just like Memory.

Here is how the game works. In Go Fish each player is given five cards. The rest of the cards are spread out in the middle of all the players, face down. These face down cards are the fish. The goal of the game is to get the most matching cards.

You hold your five cards in your hand so that only you can see them. There is no peeking at any other player's cards. You start the game by taking turns and asking other players if they have a certain card that you need to get a match. For example, you have a card in your hand that has a cat on it. You ask someone else who is playing (you can ask anyone) if they have a card with a cat on it. If they do not then you must Go Fish. If they do have a card with a cat on it, they must give you that card and you get another turn. If you have to Go Fish this means you must pick a card from the pile in front of all of you. If the card you pick matches another card you already have, then you get to have another turn. If the card does not match any of the cards you have, you keep that card in your hand and it is the next persons turn. You only get more than one turn if you get a match. The player with the most matching cards once all the cards are matched is the winner.

Memory and Go Fish are just two examples of card games that you and the kids can play. There are many other card games available. Take some time to see what else is out there and remember you can always invent your own card games.

Video Games And Television
(ages = all)
(for one or more children)

Many kids love to play video games and watch TV. Personally I think there are better activities that you and the children can do other than sitting in front of a computer or TV screen. If you and the kids do play video games and watch TV, keep in mind a few things. First, make sure the game or the TV program that you are watching or playing is geared towards the children. Most games and TV programs are rated just like a movie. If a game or TV program is not rated for children or you do not think they should be playing or watching it, then do not allow them to play or view. Many games and TV shows are violent and contain inappropriate language.

However, there are some games and TV shows that are educational for kids, keep in mind that not all video games and TV shows are offensive.

Video games tend to cause problems regarding who will play them, what games they will play, and how long they will be able to play. If any of these arguments come up then you should set a time limit that allows each child to play for five or ten minutes. If this does not work, then suggest that they play something else instead of video games. This goes for the TV as well. If you all can not decide what to watch, then don't watch anything at all. Real games are more fun any way.

Action Figures And Dolls
(ages = all)
(for one or more children)

Kids often play with either action figures or dolls on a regular basis. If the ones who you are babysitting do, play along with them. You can have make-believe adventures with the action figures or have the dolls talk and make up a variety of stories. The possibilities are endless when dealing with action figures and dolls. These toys are simple and most kids usually have them on hand. Have fun with these simple and common toys.

Puzzles
(ages = all)
(for one or more children)

Puzzles, like action figures and dolls, are common in most child-friendly homes. There are, however, many different types of puzzles. Some are geared towards very young children and have large pieces that fit together easily, while some puzzles are made for older kids and have many tiny pieces on which a younger child could easily choke. When playing with puzzles be certain the kids who are playing are the appropriate age for the puzzle. Most boxes will give a certain age range for the children who should be using these toys.

There are also many different pictures on puzzles. Some will be of flowers and mountains and some will be pictures of the kid's favorite cartoon characters. Pick a puzzle that is appropriate for the child, that way they will have more fun playing with it. When playing with puzzles make sure you find a safe area that is large enough to fit the entire puzzle. A kitchen table, for example, is usually a logical place to put together a puzzle.

Have Them Create Games
(ages = all)
(for one or more children)

Always remember that most kids have very active imaginations. If you do not know what to do with them, or you need more ideas, have the kids create their own games. This can be special and exciting. You never know what the kids might come up with. If the game works well, write down how you played it and what the rules are so next time you run out of ideas you can play this game again.

Another way that will help the children to make up their own games is by asking them questions. Ask them what they and their friends do for amusement. If they like to play house, then fabricate a story about the house that you have and invite the kids into your imaginary house. If they like playing board games, then design your own rules to a common board game. You can also make up riddles and jokes. Even if the kid's jokes do not make much sense or are not funny, it is always polite to laugh at the jokes and encourage them to tell more. Use your imagination when creating games and, you never know, you may invent a new game that children everywhere will love to play!

Pets
(ages = two and up, depending on the animal and the children)
(for one to three children depending on the animal and the children)

Pets can transform a routine day into a special day. With any animal, the potential for danger is available. If you are going to be playing with a pet make sure that the kids are familiar with the animal and that the animal is familiar and comfortable with the kids. Also, it is crucial that the animals belong to the kids. Don't allow them to play with stray or unknown animals, even if they have seen the animal in the neighborhood before. These animals may have diseases and may injure the children. One type of animal that is very safe and entertaining, especially for younger kids, are fish. A fish swimming in a fishbowl can keep a child occupied for hours of calm and enjoyable entertainment.

When you are playing with pets always be vigilant. Don't allow them to be too rough with the pets and always keep an eye on them. If you do not trust the pet, find something else to do with the kids and leave the animal alone.

Books
(ages = any)
(for one or more children)

Books are always entertaining and useful to keep kids occupied. Most homes have plenty of books lying around; most youngsters have favorite books that they love to read over and over again. If a child wants you to read them a book, have them pick out the book. This will provide the child with the satisfaction of being in control of the situation which will make them easier to deal with.

When you start to read the book add in a few different words once in a while. Change the story around on them. Have it be silly. Chances are the kid will catch you doing these changes and they will challenge you. Now you have the opportunity to have some more giggles with the child. You can point at the pictures and argue your version of the story, while the child will give you their version of the story. This interactive book reading will make reading time more enjoyable for both of you.

You can also look at picture books together. Ask the kids questions about the pictures. You can ask them what color a certain item is, or how many birds are in a certain tree. Ask questions that describe what both of you are viewing. This type of "reading" will allow the child to learn something and will help teach them to use their imagination. Using your imaginations can also make a book that you have read a thousand times seem much more interesting.

Act Out Books
(ages = any)
(for one or more children)

If you or the child wants to take books a step farther, act them out. Have the child act out one part of the book and you or another sibling can demonstrate another. This will offer the child the opportunity to be creative. Once you are prepared, you can then perform an entire show about the book.

Songs & Music
(ages = any)
(for one or more children)

Many children know numerous songs and enjoy music. Ask them if they play an instrument. Talk to them about their favorite music groups. Have them show you their cd's. You might discover that these kids know more about music than you did at their age. They might be able to sing a song for you, do a dance or play an instrument. If they do, act as if it is the best thing that you have ever heard or seen. Clap for them and praise them as good musicians and performers. This will really create a good impression on the child and will pass some time quickly and enjoyably.

It is sometimes helpful to have music playing in the background as you play other games with the kids. If they hear music they will feel more secure in their surroundings. Also, if the children are getting rowdy, playing some soft music may calm them down.

Some examples of all time favorite children's songs are the Alphabet Song, Hush Little Baby, Twinkle Twinkle Little Star and Row Row Row Your Boat. Some tapes or cd's that the children have may contain these songs and many more.

Snack Time Fun
(ages = all)
(for one or more children)

You will most likely need to feed the children that you are babysitting a snack at some time. When the kids are hungry don't just feed them snacks, make it memorable. There are many different things that you can do with snack time and food that will make eating much more pleasant.

First, find out what type of food the kids feel like eating. Search through the cupboards and give them a variety of options. Some good snack items are fruit, crackers, cheese, popsicles, juice, cereal, vegetables and other items that are easy to prepare, eat and clean up. Once they have made their food selections the fun begins.

Here are some ideas of what you can do with snack time to make it special:

• **Have a picnic**
  You can set a blanket down on the ground outside or inside in a safe and clean area. The kitchen floor will do fine. Have the children put their food on a plate and then all of you sit down and eat. You can tell them that they are all on a mini picnic together. Most kids love

picnics and this will let them use their imagination about their own picnic in their house.

You could also have a tea party. Set up the tea party like you would the picnic. With any tea party be sure you have the kids invite some of their favorite stuffed animals if they want. But don't feed the stuffed animals!

- **Have fun with the food**

  You can take crackers and design happy faces on them with cheese, carrots or most any other snack food. Have the children help you make these fun creations. You can also make ants on a log. This fun food is celery with peanut butter spread on it with raisins stuck in the peanut butter. You can also create sandwiches and use cookie cutters to form the sandwiches into unique shapes and sizes. Let them explore their own food ideas. Since these will all be snack foods there should not be much of a clean up. The possibilities are endless with snack time. Just remember to keep it simple. When you are all finished, have the kids help you clean up which can also be fun.

Arts And Crafts
(ages = all)
(for one or more children)

The subject of arts and crafts is almost infinite. There are so many different kinds of arts and crafts that you can construct, play with and cook with that there are whole books on the subject. I'm just going to go over a few ideas that you might want attempt. But, like anything else there are always more ideas out there and you can be creative and design your own masterpieces.

When doing arts and crafts always remember that not everyone is creative. Some kids love making things while it is difficult for others to even draw a circle. Also, younger kids tend to have more trouble with craft type things than older kids do. When planning a craft always keep in mind the age and skills of the child. If you do not know their skill level, then start with a simple activity such as coloring and see how they do. From there you can build up to more complex projects.

Safety is a major issue in arts and crafts. Only use items that you know the kids can handle. For example, don't let them use scissors or glue if you don't think they will be safe. Here are some rules to follow when making arts and crafts.

Rule 1—Always find a safe and clean area where you can design your crafts. This area could be inside or outside. When dealing with paint, glue, or other messy supplies, make sure there is a covering such as newspaper or a plastic sheet between the workplace and the craft. You don't want to ruin a nice table or floor.

Rule 2—Follow all safety guidelines of the supplies that you are using. Don't let the kids eat the glue, paint or any other items. Avoid using things on which the kids might choke. This includes tiny buttons, coins, and other small items. Never do crafts while the kids are eating. You don't want them eating their art instead of their food.

Rule 3—Keep all supplies off the floor and out of the reach of pets and small children. Pets and small children can make a mess of your supplies as well as becoming ill or choking if they eat any of them.

Rule 4—When you are finished making your creations be sure you and the kids clean up. You should tidy the entire area that you made the arts and crafts as well as clean the kids and yourself off.

Art and craft supplies that you may need:

This is a partial list of different supplies that you may want to have available for the kids to use. It is best to only get out the supplies that you will use. This cuts down on the mess and there will be less clean up.

You can use paper plates, safety scissors, crayons, paper, pens, glue, a safe area to work, popsicle sticks, stickers, markers, string, glitter, clay, empty egg cartons, balloons, cereal (for crafts, not eating), pinecones, cookie cutters, coloring books and any other supplies that you may need and that you think are safe for your crafts.

Some arts and crafts ideas:

- **Puppets**
  Puppets may be created from a variety of materials. You could have the kids color a face on a paper plate and then glue a popsicle stick to the plate as a handle for the puppet. You could also decorate an old sock and put your hand in the sock and have the sock puppet move. You could even build fancy puppets called marionettes out of papier-mâché and strings if you are creative enough and have the time.

  Puppets are fun because kids of almost any age can create some type of puppet and the types of puppets that you can make are almost limitless.

- **Postcards**
  Postcards are always fun to create. All you need is a small postcard-sized piece of paper, some supplies and an active imagination. You can have the kids decorate their postcard in different styles and colors. They can write a note to their parents about how much fun they are having with you. Once they are finished creating their postcard, you can play make-believe and be a mail carrier and deliver them their letters.

- Jewelry

  There are actual jewelry kits that you can buy where the kids can create neat earrings, bracelets, and necklaces. You can make simple jewelry with string and other supplies such as popcorn, cereal, hard pasta, beads and straws. You can help the kids take the string and thread it through the supplies so that they can create all different types of necklaces and bracelets.

- Drawing

  All the youngsters need is paper, something to draw with, and an imagination. Depending on the child's ability they may be able to draw fancy pictures or simple scribbles. Regardless of their ability, drawing is always entertaining. Some ideas of things to draw are the family pet, a family picture, a picture of themselves, a picture of their house as well as anything else that they may think of.

- Clay

  Make sure that the clay is kept in a safe area because it can be messy. When playing with clay have the kids roll up their shirtsleeves and wear old shirts or aprons that can get dirty if necessary. Then help the kids create a statue or any shape that they can think of. The possibilities with clay are endless, but it can be very, very messy.

- Holiday crafts

  You may be babysitting during a particular holiday. If you are then try to have the arts and crafts reflect the holiday. If it is Christmas time, maybe you can draw Christmas trees with the kids. If it is Hanukkah, you and the kids can make dradels. Before you start making holiday crafts find out what holidays the kids and family celebrate.

These are just a few examples of different arts and crafts that you and the kids can play. As you will find out, there are tons more things that you can do with arts and crafts. Have fun exploring different ideas and activities. Also, ask the kids what arts and crafts they enjoy doing. They may have a favorite craft that they can teach you!

GAMES YOU CAN PLAY
...OUTSIDE

These games are all games that should be played outside. Before you play any of these games you need to designate a certain area that the game will be played. When playing games outside you must always closely watch the children. There are more chances of them getting out of your sight outside compared to inside.

Freeze Tag
(ages = two and up, depending on their ability to run and play)
(for four or more children)

This is an entertaining game that is as much fun to play, as it is to watch. In this case, you should be the one watching to make sure the kids are playing safely and by the rules.

The rules are simple, one person is "it" and it is their job to tag the other players who are trying to avoid being tagged. When they tag another player that player must freeze in place. They are frozen until another player, not the person who is "it," touches them. Now the frozen person is unfrozen. The game is over when the person who is "it" freezes all the other players. When this happens pick someone else to be it and play again.

Statues
(ages = all)
(for two or more children)

Statues is the same as Sleeping Lions which is a game to play inside. The only difference between these two games is that when playing statues the players are standing up frozen, instead of lying down.

Statues is simple. All the players must stand frozen like a statue. If they move they are out. The last statue standing still wins.

Simon Says
(ages = two and up)
(for two or more children)

This classic game is always fun. You are "Simon." The participants need to do whatever you do only if you say, "Simon says…"and then the command. For example, if you say, "Simon says raise your right hand," all the players must raise their right hand. If anyone does not raise their right hand they are out.

If "Simon" says, "Raise your right hand" and does not say the phrase "Simon Says" and someone raises their right hand, they will be out. Only when Simon says, "Simon says…" and then gives a command the players act upon that command. If Simon does not say "Simon says" and a participant does the action, they are out. The last person remaining is the winner.

Chalk
(ages = all)
(for one or more children)

This is not really a game but an activity. It is fun to take pieces of chalk and draw on the driveway, sidewalk or on a chalkboard. This is a good activity to do only if the area you will be drawing in is safe. Before you and the children begin to draw make sure that there will not be any cars coming up the driveway if you are drawing outside near the driveway.

The kids may draw pictures, words, hopscotch courses, and anything else. This is especially enjoyable to do on a bright sunny day. When you have all completed drawing you can leave the art there or wash it off with water from a hose, bucket or use an eraser for a chalkboard.

Piggyback Rides
(ages = all)
(for one child at a time)

A piggyback ride is when a child climbs on your back and you carry them around. Before you give any little ones rides on your back you must be able to carry the child easily. If you can carry them on your back, but not easily, then do not give them a piggyback ride. I recommend that you give a child a piggyback ride only if you can pick them up with little or no effort. You should give only one child a ride at a time.

Be sure you do not wear yourself out too much when giving piggyback rides. If you are getting tired or light headed, take a rest.

Bubbles
(ages = all)
(for one or more children)

Bubbles is one of the few activities that can really be enjoyed by kids of all ages. Blowing bubbles is safe, entertaining, and harmless. The chance of having an accident with bubbles is slim unless you spill them on the ground and then slip on the bubble mix. If you do spill the bubble mix, clean it up and continue to play. And once you are done playing with bubbles make sure you clean up. Bubble can become messy if they are not washed away with water.

There are many different types of bubble blowing devices. There are bubble guns that can continuously blow bubbles at a rapid pace. There are also bubble blowers that can blow many different size bubbles at once. There are even bubble blowers that can create giant bubbles that are tons of fun. The only cautions when dealing with bubbles is that you must ensure that the children do not drink the bubbles, get them in their eyes and that they play with them in a safe area. Other than that bubbles are a great way to entertain kids.

Forts
(ages = all ages)
(for one or more children)

Building a fort is a very easy and fun activity for kids of any and all ages. They can use old boxes, sheets, blankets or any other material to build a really great fort. Be sure that they are constructed in a safe area and that the children don't use any tools or unsafe materials. A good fort can be as simple as draping a sheet or towel over a tree branch or chair. Once the fort is complete you and the children can play games in it.

Bikes And Trikes
(ages = two and up ensuring that that can ride a bike or tricycle)
(for no more then four kids)

Most children love riding bicycles, tricycles, and scooters. If they want to ride them when you are there make sure that their parents said it is okay. Find out where they can and can not ride their bikes. Maybe they can only ride them in the driveway or in a certain park. If the kids go bike riding, make sure you go with them and that all of you wear helmets and other safety equipment—it's the law. If there are not enough helmets for all of you, then none of you should go bike riding. You also need to know how adept the children are at riding a bike. If one child is not very good then it is better not to let any of the kid's ride. With bikes you all need to stick together. You never know when one of the kids or yourself may fall off and get hurt.

When riding bikes in a safe area with the proper equipment you can set up obstacles for the youngsters to go around such as cones. Always make safety your number one priority. Bike injuries can be serious. If you think the kids might get hurt then don't go bike riding.

Red Light, Green Light
(ages = various, ability to walk and listen to directions)
(for two or more children)

This is an entertaining game to play with any number of children. The rules are simple. One person is the "light." The "light's" job is to run the game.

First, line up all the participants at a designated starting line. Then designate a finish line such as a tree, or an object that is not too far away. The "light" stands at the finish line. Then the game begins. The "light" yells out "green light," and the participants walk toward the finish line. Then once the "light" yells out "red light" all the participants must freeze. If any of them keeps moving, they return to the starting line. The game continues with "red lights" and "green lights" being called out until there is a winner who is the first person to cross the finish line. The winner then becomes the new "light" and the game starts over.

Hop Scotch
(ages = three and up depending on ability)
(for one or more children)

This classic game is always fun to play. All you need is some chalk and the creativity of making a hop scotch course which consists of different squares connected together where the participants hop from square to square. You can make up you own rules in this game or use the traditional rules where you throw a stone on one of the squares. Then you can not step on that square as you hop on the course.

Jump Rope
(ages = four and up, depending on ability)
(for one or more children)

This is great outside game because it can be played almost anywhere. All you need is a jump rope and patience. This is also a good activity for children with an abundant amount of energy. To jump rope, hold one end of the rope in each hand and flip the rope around your body and jump over it. It can also be done with a longer rope where two kids jump at once and two people hold each end of the rope and turn it. See how many times the kids can do it without stopping, then have them try to beat that number.

Play Sets
(ages = three and up depending on the child)
(for one or more children)

Play sets are a good way to have lots of enjoyment and to keep youngsters occupied. You can either use a backyard play set or go to a local park or school that has slides, sand, and swings. Make sure you supervise the kids and bring along some shovels or other play things if there is sand with which to build sandcastles and other fun creations.

Public Parks
(ages = all)
(for one or more children)

Going to a public park is a treat for most children. Most parks have slides, swings, and other fun equipment to play on. Be careful when taking children to public parks. You must always keep a careful eye on them at all times. You never know who else will be at public parks and you will also be farther away from help if someone gets hurt. Only go to public parks if they are close to the kid's house and if you feel safe. If you don't feel safe for any reason go, back to the kid's home and play there.

Homework Fun

When it is time for kids to do their homework many problems may arise. Some children will tell you that they don't want to do their homework or that they do not have any homework or they will use numerous other excuses in order to avoid doing their work. The way to get them to do their homework without many problems is to turn it into a game. Before you start making homework fun you need to find out a few things.

- Do they really have homework? Ask the parents before they leave if the kids need to do any homework.

- Find out where the kids do their homework. Do they need to use a certain computer or be at a certain desk?

- Find out what the children need to do their homework. Do they need paper, pens, or a notebook?

The more you know about the kids' homework the easier it will be for you when they try to not do it. Ask the parents questions before they leave so you know exactly what you and the kids need to do. Now let's make homework fun!

There are many different techniques and games that you can use to get the children to do their homework. To follow are a few ideas.

- Do the homework together. This might not sound like much fun, but it can be. Chances are the kids' homework is something that you already know and should be easy for you. Also, the time that you will be spending together will be quality time and most kids like spending time with their babysitter. Be careful not to do their homework for them, do it with them.

- Challenge them to a homework race. This is especially useful if the children refuse to do their homework. This will get them to do a little homework, which is better than none at all. This is how it works: you do your homework and they do theirs. Who ever finishes first wins. Before you start this game you must designate a start and finish place in the child's homework. Maybe they need to read ten pages in a book or do five math problems. You also need to make it clear that you will check their work when they are finished so they must do it well. As far as your work, if you don't have any homework then make something up. Show that child that you too are busy doing work. Once you and the child are finished have them quiz you on what you did after you quiz them.

- You could also make homework entertaining for the kids by helping them with theirs. The child may not understand their work. If you help them with it, they will most likely be more enthusiastic to do it. This is different than doing it with them because when you help the child they come to you with specific questions. When you do the homework with them you and the child do all the work together. Just letting the child know that you are there to help them is often a relief.

- You can also use other tricks to get the kids to do their work. If they are really uncooperative and will not do their homework no matter what you do maybe give them a piece of candy after they are done. If the kid is still uncooperative you could also tempt them into doing their homework by limiting other activities until the work is completed. You might say that they can't play any games until the homework is finished, for example.

The bottom line for homework is that most children would rather not do it. They would much rather play a game or have a snack. When you are faced with a child who refuses to do their homework be patient. Don't get angry with them or lose your temper. Use your imagination and be creative in order to make homework time a fun time.

The most important point of games is to keep the kids and you active and most games do that. Also the children will always remember what you did and how much fun they had when you were babysitting. Chances are excellent you will be asked back again and again to babysit if the youngsters have fun. Play as many games as you can so that the children are entertained. When they have fun, you have fun. What can be better than having fun on the job?

Chapter Seven

What To Do And Not Do While Babysitting

In this chapter we will explore different things that you should and should not do while babysitting. Some of the things discussed here are common sense items, while other topics may not be so common. If you do a poor job or make a bad decision while babysitting, then chances are you will not find many more jobs in the future. Don't take any extra chances while babysitting.

The most important thing that you can do while babysitting is create a great first impression, which was discussed earlier. The next important thing that you need to do while babysitting is create a great last impression. When you are finished babysitting and leave the house, you need to be sure that the parents, children and yourself are comfortable and satisfied with the job that you did. You need to be courteous and smile as you leave the house.

Here is a list of things that you should do while babysitting:

—Do have fun. Your primary function as a babysitter is the keep the kids safe and to entertain them. Playing games and keeping everyone active is definitely something that you should do.

—Do play fair. You are there to babysit the kids not to beat them in games. Don't cheat or play too rough or competitively in any games or activities.

—Do follow the rules that the parents left for you and the children. You want to make sure that you do everything to the best of your ability and do what the parents want you to do. They have certain rules for a reason and it is your job to respect their rules in their house for their children. If you do not agree about a certain rule that a parent has left for you and the kids then you can discuss it with them before or after you babysit. Do not ignore a rule just because you do not like it.

—Do eat. If you are hungry then eat. Many times babysitters will not eat the food that is offered to them. It is much easier to babysit on a full stomach then on an empty one. Don't be shy when it comes to food. If you don't like what food there is search for something else. Chances are pretty good that you will always find something that you like.

—Do clean up after yourself. If you and the kids create a mess, then take the time to clean up whatever mess you made. It is also wise to do a little extra cleaning if you find the time. Anything extra that you do will be greatly appreciated by the parents.

—Do manage your time. Many times while babysitting you will need to get things completed by a certain time. You may need to pick one child up at practice, feed them or get them to bed by a certain time. Always glance at your watch and make sure you get everything completed on time, or at least as close as you can.

—Do dress appropriately. If it is cold out, wear a jacket. You don't want to wear torn clothing or clothing that is not appropriate for babysitting. You need to be comfortable, not grubby.

—Do be safe. Make sure everything that you and the youngsters do is safe. This includes playing safely, eating safely, and being safe at whatever else you do. Safety is your number one concern.

This list of Do's will give you some idea of what you should do when babysitting. Of course, there are always more things that you should do, but always use your common sense.

Now here is a list of things you should not do while babysitting.

—Do not have your friends over while you are babysitting. You are there to watch the kids, not to play with your friends.

—Do not leave the children alone for any reason. If you need to go somewhere in an emergency, take the kids with you.

—Do not talk on the phone unless it is absolutely necessary. You need to watch the kids, not talk to your friends.

—Do not talk to strangers. These could be people coming to the door or strangers at public parks or other areas.

—Don't panic. If you are having a hard time babysitting do not give up. Do your best. If you have a problem with a child, call their parents or tell their parents what happened when they return.

—Do not steal. This includes taking things from the house or from the children. If you steal then you will most likely never get a job again and you could be arrested.

—Do not lie. This includes lying to the parents and to the kids. If you lie then chances are someone will find out and you will get in trouble and lose your job

—Do not use drugs. This is pretty self-explanatory. Drugs include smoking, chewing tobacco, drinking alcohol, and using other illegal narcotics or drugs.

—Do not use inappropriate words and language. Anything you say could and will most likely be repeated by the kids to their parents or other children. Watch what you say and what you tell the children. There is no place for foul language especially around kids.

—Do not attempt to hide anything from the parents. If you or the children break something in the house, let the parents know. It is better to be honest and straightforward then to hide something and be dishonest. If you do try to hide something, chances are the parents will eventually find out and you will lose your job.

These two lists of what you should and should not do while babysitting are not meant to scare or deter you in any way from babysitting. You must understand that there are certain things that you should and should not do. This goes for any job, not just babysitting. If you do find yourself in a tricky situation where you are not sure what to do, take a few seconds to think things over. Remember, every parent was once your age and they know what it is like to be young. Trust yourself and always strive to do the honest and respectable thing no matter what the situation may be.

Chapter Eight

What About...

This chapter "What About..." addresses many common questions and concerns that babysitters face or will face as they babysit more and more. These issues will help you better prepare yourself for any situation that may arise. Most of us, for example, have never changed a diaper or had to give a child a bath. This section will give you step by step approaches in dealing with certain situations that will most definitely come up as you babysit.

What about...
Diapers

This is a dirty subject that you will inevitably have to face. Follow these simple directions, keep your hopes up and most importantly don't forget to smile.

First of all, there are many different types of diapers. There are cloth diapers, disposable diapers, and diapers that come in different sizes. Find out what type of diaper the child uses. Ask the parents to demonstrate diaper changing if this is new for you. Sometimes, if you are only babysitting for a short time, you won't need to change the child's diaper. If you do, follow these simple steps and it will be easy.

Changing a diaper:

Checklist
—diapers
—baby wipes

—changing table or a blanket on the floor
—clean clothes

Step 1—Collect all the necessary items that you will need to change the baby. The items from the checklist above may all be necessary.

Step 2—Take the child into the designated changing area. This is a safe area that the parents designate as the changing area. This area could be a blanket or towel on the floor or on an actual changing table. You may

want to change a baby on a bed or a sofa. Always keep one hand on the baby to prevent them from rolling off. Some changing tables will have straps or safety restraints that hold the baby in place. If the table does have straps, then gently strap the baby down so they can not move away. If there are no straps make sure you always keep your eyes and hands on the baby at all times.

Step 3—Remove the dirty diaper. Most diapers have a tape like substance at the hips of the baby on the diaper. Gently pull the tape apart to remove the diaper. If the diapers have safety pins, carefully remove the pins and make sure you do not prick yourself or the child. Once you remove the diaper either throw it away in the designated trash area for diapers or move it to the side and throw it away once you are finished changing the child.

As you are changing the baby it is a good idea to keep them occupied. Talk to the little one and give them a toy to hold.

Step 4—Lift the baby's hips off the changing surface by gently holding the baby by the ankles with one finger between them so they do not rub and so you keep in control. If the baby starts to slip, just relax your grip and have a go at it again.

Step 5—Gently wipe the baby with some baby wipes especially if the diaper is messy. You will want to wipe girls front to back.

Step 6—Now use a damp cloth or another baby wipe to clean the whole diaper area of the baby. Make sure you get all the creases in the skin and especially around the genital area. Be sure to be gentle when you are wiping a baby.

Step 7—Lift the baby's hips off the changing table once again and slide the clean diaper under the baby's bottom.

Step 8—Pull the diaper between the legs and pin or tape it in place. Most diapers have tape already inside them. To get to the tape gently pull the tabs apart on the end of the diaper. If you are using pins make sure you place your hand between the diaper and the baby's skin. You do not want to accidentally stick the baby with the pin.

Step 9—Place the baby in a safe place once the diaper is on him or her. Then place any appropriate clothing on the baby. When you dress a child always be careful of their arms and legs and of any zippers that could get caught in their skin.

What about…
Baths

Checklist
—toys
—tear free shampoo (Babies do not need soap or shampoo. It can dry out their skin. Clean water is good enough.)
—towels
—portable phone

Baths can be a very challenging event if you are not prepared. Follow these simple instructions to ensure a fun filled bathing experience.

- First, make sure you have plenty of bath toys that will not hurt the kid's feet if they step on them or toys that they could choke on. These toys will help keep the children occupied as you wash behind their ears and scrub their feet.

- Second, make sure you use tear free shampoo. This will eliminate any potentially painful baths.

- Make sure that you have plenty of bath towels handy when the kids are in the bath. Once they are finished they will want to dry off. If the towels are not readily available you may lose one of the kids as they bolt around the house, soaking wet and naked.

- Keep a portable telephone in the bathroom, if possible. This should be used in emergencies if you need to call for help. You should never leave the children alone in the bathroom or tub if the phone rings. If you do not have a portable phone, allow the phone to ring. Never ever leave a child in a tub.

Baths get easier with practice. Be patient and pay attention to what you are doing. Chances are you will also get wet from the bath water. Some children relish baths while others despise them. Be prepared.

What about...
Bottles

Some children take a bottle while others do not. The bottle can be a very significant thing for a child who needs it to go to sleep. It can be a security item that will calm them down. If the bottle is not ready when they are, you may have an unhappy child on your hands. Always ask their parents if the child needs a bottle. If they do take a bottle, find out where it is and how to prepare it. A bottle is a good thing to soothe a cranky or upset child.

What about...
Naptime

Naptime can be quite an experience. Some kids love to take naps while others utterly despise it. If you babysit a child who hates naps here are a few tips to try to get the child to nap.

- First, give the child advance warning before it is naptime. Ask them what they would like to do before their nap. This could be playing a game, taking a walk, or some other activity. This will hopefully eliminate any excuse they may use when it is naptime.

- Second, get their bed ready for them before they get in it. This will stop any stalling techniques that the child may attempt to use. You might also read a book to the child as they crawl into bed. This book will hopefully soothe and relax the child.

- Third, close the blinds and turn off the lights to set the nighttime mood. Once they are in bed, close the door, and give them a few minutes where you listen to them in the room. They may try to get out of the room or start to cry or fuss. If they get out of bed, go in and put them back. Tell them they need a nap to grow up big and strong. If they cry, you have to leave them in bed crying. This will be hard for you to do, but it is the best way to deal with a crying child. After a few minutes of crying the child will most probably stop crying and fall asleep.

What about...
Bedtime

Checklist
—bottle
—special stuffed animals
—bed time story
—plenty of blankets

Bedtime, like naptime can be quite challenging. Some children will easily go to bed while others will be more difficult.

• First, you must find out from the parents what time is bedtime. Find out where the children sleep, what they wear to bed, what do they need to do before they go to bed (brush their teeth, drink a bottle), do the lights stay on or do they need a night light, and do the children follow a particular bedtime ritual.

One problem that comes up with bedtime is stalling. Some children will seek to waste as much time as they can. They will brush their teeth slowly, walk slowly, get dressed slowly and use any and all other tactics they can to stall their bed time. The way to get around this is to get them ready for bed sooner. Even one hour earlier could be necessary depending on the kids. Bedtime will vary per person and the only true way to get in the pattern of what happens is to just do it.

What about...
Where They Sleep

Finding the right place for the kids to sleep can be baffling. Their parents tell you that they sleep in their beds. Then once it is bedtime, the kids tell you that they sleep in their parent's bed or another place. If this happens let the children sleep where they want unless it is in a dangerous place. You can either move them to their appropriate sleeping place once they fall asleep, or tell their parents where they are sleeping when they get home and they can move them.

What about...
All Day Babysitting

All day babysitting is when you babysit for a longer period of time than a normal job. The key to having a successful all day babysitting job is three things: food, organization, and fun. You need to have enough variety of foods for breakfast, lunch, dinner, and snacks. This means that every meal needs to be different and prepared or organized by you. Find out exactly what food they have in the house and where it is.

You also need to be organized. When you babysit the whole day the children may need to be somewhere and you may need to either drive them or coordinate rides to get them there. It is a good idea for the parents to create lists for all day babysitting telling you who, what, when, how, and where something needs to be completed. You should follow these lists as best you can to ensure that everyone gets where they are supposed to be on time.

The most important key to all day babysitting is keeping the kids entertained. You need to keep the children occupied and busy the whole day. The best way to do this is by playing a variety of games that are all unique. You should play a very active game for a while and then play a quiet game. Keep them involved and interested. Sometimes all day babysitting may become boring or overwhelming. The best way to counteract that is by keeping active and playing games.

When the parents return from being gone all day you may want to give them a brief review of everything that you and the children did. Chances are there may have been a few things that did not go as scheduled, which is fine just as long as you let the parents know. If you can get through an all day babysitting job smiling the whole time, then this is the job for you!

What about...
Overnight Babysitting

Some time in your babysitting career you may be asked to babysit overnight. This means that you will sleep over at someone else's house and wake up with the kids, alone. This can be a very scary experience if you are not prepared. Before you take on this endeavor make sure you know and get along with the kids and parents very well. I don't recommend overnight babysitting for someone your first time that you babysit for these people unless you feel comfortable with your babysitting skills and the family once you meet them. Also, you need to know what to do in the morning. Do the children need to be somewhere in the morning? Do they eat a certain breakfast? What time are the parents going to be coming back? You also need to know where the parents are going, and what special things need to get done that would not go along with a "normal" babysitting job.

What about...
After School Babysitting

After school babysitting is when you arrive at the home before the children do and the parents are not there. This type of babysitting usually lasts only until the parents get home from work. When you do this type of babysitting you first need to have a way to get in the house. You should either have a key or know where one is hidden. Once you are in the house look around to check that everything is in its place and that there are not any dangerous or potentially dangerous items lying around. If there are, clean them up. Then wait for the children to come home.

When the kids come home you should greet them and offer them a snack. The snack should be simple snack foods that are easy to clean up. Once they have finished their snack they can change into play clothes and now it is playtime. You may also need to get the kids to soccer practice or other activities at this time. If you do, make sure you know who goes where, when they go and how they get there and back. Many parents will leave a list for this type of babysitting. You need to read the list.

Once playtime is over you may need to prepare the kids' dinner or have them work on homework. Check with the children to see if they have any homework and if they say no, then read a book with them. You may also want to help them with their homework if they need it. By this time the parents may have returned home. When they get home greet them and tell them what you and their children did. Then you will get paid and will be on your way.

After school babysitting is usually very easy. You do not need to put the children to bed and most of the time the kids will already be tired out from a long day at school. Enjoy after school babysitting if you ever get the chance to do it.

What about…
Babysitting For More Than One Family At The Same Time

Many times when you babysit, parents with children may be going to the same place together. In this case you may be asked to babysit for two or more sets of kids at once. Before you agree to this sometimes-chaotic task ask a few questions.

- First, ask how many children you will be babysitting and what their ages are.

- Second, ask if the children get along with each other.

- Third, ask where you will be watching these children.

- Fourth, ask about the pay before you start. The more children you babysit at one time, the more the pay should be.

If you ask these questions, and get satisfactory answers, try this type of babysitting. It could lead to many more jobs if you take good care of the kids.

What about...
Rainy And Snowy Days

You might be babysitting one day and it starts to snow or rain. Now what do you do? Some kids like to play in the rain. This means mud and dirt for you. Other children are scared of the rain. This means a frightened child to deal with. Snow may present many problems such as slipping on ice or getting frostbite. If you don't want the kids to go out in bad weather, then keep them busy inside. Play games with them. Keep them away from windows so they don't see what is going on outside. This way you don't need to talk a child out of going into the rain and the mud. However, if you don't mind a muddy child, and you have discussed this with the children's parents and they don't mind a muddy child, by all means go out and have fun and be safe in the rain, mud and snow.

What about...
Food

CHECK LIST
—food for you
—special diets
—money for food
—snacks

Food is a very crucial part of babysitting. You need to eat and the children need to eat. Ask the parents what the kids should eat if you need to fix them dinner or a snack. Always ask if they are on a special or restricted diet. Also, sometimes religious or other practices may come into play with food. If in doubt, ask.

Many times parents leave money for you to decide what to do for food. The best way to avoid any potential bickering about what to eat is to create a game out of it.

- First, make a list of possibilities. For example, you could add food such as pizza, Chinese food, chicken and other foods. Write them down. Then give the options to the kids. Have them vote on what they want. If there is not a majority then write down the most popular choices onto a small piece of paper and pick one out of a hat. This will be the place that you will eat. If one child does not like the result, order the food anyway. When it gets there, and if they are hungry, they will eat. If they fuss about it don't worry if they do not eat. Make sure you let them know that the food is for them. If they don't eat, it is their choice and you do not need to worry about it.

Snack time can also be an ordeal. You need to ask the parents what snacks are allowed and how much is allowed. Once the limit is reached then put them away. If the kids fuss, change the subject. If they continue to fuss and attempt to get the food, put it in a place they can't reach. Make sure they don't know where you put it. You don't need a child trying to climb on the cupboards or tables where they can get hurt or break something.

The bottom line on food is to find out what the children prefer. Communicate with the children and offer them choices, but never force-feed them. Force-feeding a child will make your job more difficult and will give the children a bad impression of you.

What about...
Medicines

This is simple, but could be deadly. If the kids need to take medicine make sure you are alerted by their parents before hand. You need to know what type of medicine, how much and how often it needs to be taken. If the children tell you that they need to take a certain medicine and their parents did not say anything about it, don't let them take the medicine, or call their parents and ask them if possible. If the parents are not available and the child is really sick, call your parents, the doctor, or a hospital.

What about...
Security Blankets

Some children may have an item such as a blanket, pacifier, stuffed animal or other item that is so special to them that they never let it go. These items are usually called security blankets because the child feels safe and secure when they are with it. If you babysit for a child who has a security blanket do not take this item away from the child even if it is dirty or causing problems with a game or other activity. It is better to let the child hold onto these things than to take them away. If you take away a security blanket from a child they may become very angry or sad. If you are concerned about the security blanket talk to the child's parents about it. Most kids will grow away from the need for a security blanket as they get older.

What about...
Pets

Many families have pets. These pets vary from fish, cats, dogs and even snakes or turtles. When dealing with pets you may need to worry about playing with pets, feeding, and caring for pets and maybe dealing with lost pets. The general rule for playing with pets is not to do it while you are babysitting. Many pets, even if they are the children's and are the cutest things in the whole world, can still bite and have diseases. Animals that you and the children know can still bite and hurt you. Also, smaller children tend to be hurt more often by animal's than larger people. If the family does have animals, leave the animals alone. Do not attempt to play with them and do not pull their tails or be mean to them. There are plenty other activities and games that you and the kids can do that do not involve pets.

Feeding the pets is a different matter. Chances are you will have to feed a dog or cat sometime in your babysitting career. If you do need to feed a pet find out from the parents what type of food they are fed, how much food, where they are fed and how often. If you can, have them show you what to do. Many pets are on special diets and some may even be on medications, ask questions.

If the family pet is lost or runs away while you are babysitting it is not the end of the world. The first thing to do is to not panic. Most animals are fairly intelligent and if they do get out of the house chances are they will return home when they are ready. Be patient and wait for the pet to return on its own. If it does not return right away you can search the house for it. If you can not find it then wait for a while. Do not go around the neighborhood looking for the animal and do not worry too much. Tell the parents when they get home that the pet ran away. They may call the dogcatcher or the local humane society to see if the animal was found. Most animals will return home on their own.

What about...
Cleaning

If you or the children create a mess, clean it up. It is especially important to clean up after meals and snacks because bugs and other animals may be attracted to the food. It is equally important to clean up after playing because toys can cause injury if they are lying around. When you clean all of you should do it together. This means that you and the children will clean at the same time. The general rule for cleaning is to attempt to make the house appear better than the way it was when you started your babysitting job that day. Get the children in the habit of cleaning up after themselves. If they have finished playing with a toy, have them put it away before they get out another one. If you keep the house clean then it will be safer and more organized, which will make your job easier, and most parents' appreciate returning to a clean house.

Also, avoid using chemical cleaners if you can. These can be poisonous and can be very harmful to you, the kids and family pets if they are eaten, swallowed or touch your skin. Be careful.

What about...
"Older" Kids

When you babysit older children, above ten years or so, you may run into some problems because of the closeness in your age to theirs. The best way to avoid any conflict with these older kids is to not tell them your age. This is a simple plan that will hopefully avoid any conflict. If the older child does know your age and is upset about that, give them some room. Allow them do their own thing and don't hound them to do certain tasks or jobs. Concentrate on the other children in the family (if there are any) or tell their parents about any problem that may have come up. Don't worry about getting these older children to do what you want. Their parents will more than likely be aware of the situation. However do not allow them to do anything harmful or dangerous.

What about...
Friends Over...

...Yours

You should avoid having your peers over when you are babysitting. You need to focus on the youngsters. When in doubt, see your friends while you are not working. Also, don't talk to your friends on the phone when you are babysitting. You never know when the kid's parents or someone else with significant information may be calling.

...Theirs

Sometime while you are babysitting, friends of your charges may come over asking to play. You should not allow any of the kids under your

supervision to go over to anyone else's house unless it has been previ-
ously arranged with both children's parents before you start babysitting.
Also, prohibit any other children to play in the house without previous
arrangements. It is always better to turn away a friend rather than admit
them into the house and add another child to be watched.

What about...
Sick Kids

You may need to babysit for ill children. Be sure you ask their parents
what, if any, types of medicines they are allowed to take and how much.
Do not allow a child to take any medicine without a parent's consent no
matter what they might say or what medicine it is. Also, use common
sense when dealing with a sick child. Don't permit them to abuse you
with their illness. You are not there to serve them; you are there to care
for them. There is a difference. Your job is to make sure the sick child is
all right. You don't need to focus all of your attention on them and neg-
lect other kids or the house as a whole.

What if a child gets sick when you are
babysitting them? (First Aid is discussed
in a chapter ten.) Take care of the child
as you would any other sick child. Survey
the child. Do they need a doctor or do
they need to take some time resting? In
order to decide which it is talk to the
child. Look for sure signs that they may
need medical attention such as bleeding or passing out.

If you think the child is trying to fool you to get attention try this
trick. Give them a glass of water or some juice and say it is magic.
Chances are the child will get better if they are faking an illness. They
think they got your attention and you don't need to give them any
unneeded medicines.

What about...
Kids With Special Needs

All children have different needs. Some will be more specific than others. Under special needs there are two main kinds: those kids who have some special physical need and those kids who have an emotional need. For any special need, whatever it may be, discuss it with the parents before they leave. Chances are you will feel better about what you might have to do to help the child if you know more about what needs to be done. Also, you should ask if there are any phone numbers of doctors who you can call in case of an emergency and you should also ask about any medication that you might have to give the child.

A physical need is when a child is either sick, physically challenged or injured. If a child is sick, your job is to make the child feel as comfortable as you can. This may include giving them medicines that the parents tell you are okay, preparing food for the child, giving them blankets and tending to any other needs. When babysitting a sick child make sure they are doing all right. You don't need to be their servant, but try to be sure they have everything they need. An injured child could be a child with broken limbs, cuts, bruises or other physical injuries. You tend to the child, in these cases, the same way that you tend to a sick child; make sure they have everything they need.

If you babysit for a physically challenged child they may need your assistance and understanding. Some examples of a physically challenged child is one who may be in a wheelchair or needs the assistance of crutches or leg braces. But don't be fooled, many physically challenged people are very capable of caring for themselves and others. Never underestimate what they can do. When you do babysit for a physically challenged child you should ask questions. Ask their parents what you can do, or what you need to do to help the child. Also, it helps to know any telephone numbers and names of any doctors or other people you may need to call. When dealing with physically challenged children have an open mind. Most children will talk to you about their disability. Remember that these kids are kids too. They like the same things that other children like and you should treat them just like any one else.

Some of the kids you babysit may have emotional needs. You cannot see emotional needs like you can a broken arm or leg. You might not even know that child has any emotional needs unless they or the parents concede this information to you. If the parents do tell you that their child has an emotional need you should ask them what you need to do, if anything, to help the child. Do they need medication? Do they have a certain diet? Do they need help with homework? Do they have a routine that they need to follow? Try to find out as much information that you can about the child, you should not be uncomfortable around the child. When dealing with emotional children be patient and talk to them. They too are like any other kids, so treat them like that.

What about...
Broken Items And Spills

Sometime in your babysitting career something will break or spill, guaranteed. This could be a window, a vase, a television set, a drink or a glass.

If something does brake or spill follow these tips:

- Clean up the broken or spilled item as best you can. Make sure the area is safe to walk over. If it is not, then do not permit anyone to walk over that area.

- Tell the parents about the spill or broken item. This is very important. You do not want to hide a broken item or spill from the parents even if it was cleaned up. If you do attempt to hide it that will show that you are not trustworthy and the parents will find out about the spill or broken item sooner or later. When they do, chances are they will not ask you back to babysit. If you tell them about any broken item or spill this shows the parents that you are trustworthy and a good babysitter because you tell the truth.

Broken items can be replaced or fixed, but trust is not so easy to replace. Once your trust is lost it may be impossible to regain it again. Honesty is always the best policy.

What about...
Arguments And Fights

Hopefully there will never be a serious fight between siblings or between a kid and yourself when you are babysitting. But, there will most probably be small disagreements and arguments between siblings sometime in your babysitting career. Most of the time these children will be fighting over a certain object such as a toy. When siblings do fight they might scream at each other, throw things or physically hit each other. If you find yourself in the middle of feuding siblings you need to separate them. If they are not near each other then chances are they can not do bodily harm. Give your best attempt at calming the children down. If you raise your voice above their voices then most kids will quiet down. If the children do not listen to you, separate them into different rooms. If they can not see each other or get to each other then the argument will most likely stop or calm down.

Once the feuding siblings are separated you will need to find a solution. If they are fighting over a toy, do not allow either of them to have that toy. If they are fighting about something else try to find out what that is. Once the kids are calm and the fight is over do not dwell on it. Many kids have short memories when dealing with fights. One minute they may be ready to kill one another then five minutes later they will be calm and playing together nicely. The bottom line on fights is to calm the situation as quickly as you can by separating the children and removing the items that caused the fight.

If you find yourself in a fight with a kid you are babysitting, stop fighting no matter what the topic is. You are the babysitter and you should not argue or fight with the children no matter what. If the kids are not listening to you, do your best without fighting and tell their parents about the problem. There is no reason or excuse for fighting.

What about...
Lists

Some parents write long, long, long lists for their babysitter to plan every minute of the day. When you get one of these long lists glance it over and note any meaningful information and then put it aside. You are in control, and the day will not run according to any list, guaranteed. Trust yourself and your judgment. If you get into a bind, then consult the list.

What about...
The Telephone

Some stereotypical babysitters are seen as persons who jabber on the phone the whole time with their friends. This should not be you. The telephone should only be used in emergencies. You should ask the parents if they want you to answer the phone if it rings. If they do want you to answer the phone you need to find out where the phones are located and how they work. Many phones work differently. When someone does call you should not tell the caller that you are the babysitter and that the parents are not home. If they ask for the parents simply say, "They are not available right now; may I take a message." Then get the person's name, number, and what time they called. You should keep a message pad near the phone where you can write down all the messages. You want to keep the messages organized and clear.

What about...
Television

Television is a very touchy subject. It seems that TV can cause more problems than it is worth. Many parents have very strict rules regarding their children watching television. Before you babysit ask the parents their rules. Also, use common sense when you are permitting the children to watch the television. If there is a show that is inappropriate for children, don't let them watch it. Plus the average child watches over twenty five hours of television a week. You can spend your time doing more productive activities.

This brings up another problem that the television presents. What should we watch? One child will want to watch one show while another wants to watch something else. Then you get in the middle of their argument, which can cause more conflicts. The best tip about the TV is to leave it off.

What about...
Clothing

Your clothing

When you babysit, dress appropriately. You are going to a job, so look like it. Don't dress in dirty clothing or jeans with holes in them or other sloppy attire. Wear comfortable shoes. You never know what may happen. You might need to walk to a neighbor's house or somewhere else. If you don't have shoes then your feet could be seriously hurt. Also, if it is cold, bring a jacket. It is better to be overly prepared than under prepared.

Their clothing

As far as the kids use common sense. If it is raining outside have them use an umbrella or raincoat. If it is cold, have them wear a heavy coat. You should know what they need to wear to bed. Have them get their pajamas out early so there are not disagreements or lost clothing when it is bedtime. If in doubt ask the children what they normally wear or ask their parents what they should wear.

What about...
Keys

Your keys

Keys are little things that can really ruin a babysitting job. First, make sure you keep your keys with you. This could include your house keys and car keys. The worst thing is losing your keys somewhere in the house that you are babysitting. Don't put them down anywhere or give them to the kids to play with. You may never see them again.

Their keys

Ask the parents about their house keys. What if you and the kids get locked out? Do the kids have keys? Is there a hidden key? If there is a hidden key, where is it? Also, ask if any of the neighbors have keys. If they do, find out which neighbors, and if possible meet these people so if they ever come over when you are there you do not get alarmed or scared.

What about...
Cars

If you have a car and are able to drive it to and from a babysitting job, this will make it easier for the parents. If it is easier on the parents then there is a better chance that you will get more babysitting jobs. Also, sometimes you will get paid for how much gas you use going to and from their house. Some parents may also ask you to drive their kids to different places. Before you drive them anywhere ask their parents if it is okay. Make sure you and the parents know where you are going and when you need to be there. Sometimes you may even use the family's car to take the kids different places. If you are not comfortable with driving around the children in either your or their parents' car, inform the parents ahead of time. Alternate arrangements may be made.

What about...
Car Seats

Car seats are used to keep a small child safe. There are different car seats for different sizes and ages of children. Before you put a child in a car seat check with their parents. Their parents should tell you how to put the child in the car seat, how to put the car seat in the car, and where in the car the car seat belongs. Some car seats can be tricky, be patient and read the instructions on the seat if you have to. You want to have the child be as safe as possible in the car.

Here are some car seat tips.

- Never put a car seat in the front seat. If the airbag goes off in the front seat it could seriously injure the child. Put the car seat in the back seat.

- Check the car seat for any rules or suggestions. For instance, babies less than twenty pounds have a different type of car seat than bigger kids do.

- If you are babysitting for a youngster who is less than twenty pounds their car seat should face the back of the car. These car seats are well-padded, firmly constructed car seats that are designed to stay securely attached to the seat of the car.

- For children approximately twenty to sixty pounds they sit in a car seat that faces the front of the car and has the child sitting upright in a well-padded seat. This seat also is secured to the seat of the car using the car's seat belts.

- For children sixty pounds and over and who are not quite tall enough to sit in a regular seat use a small booster seat or bucket seat in the car. The seat belt, in most cases, will hold the child and the seat securely to the seat of the car.

Putting a car seat in the car and then getting a child in the seat can take a while. Be patient and take your time as you sort out the mysteries of car seats.

What about...
Bicycles, Scooters, And Skateboards

Kids love to ride bicycles, scooters, and skateboards. If the kids want to ride these while you are babysitting make sure safety is number one. Check with their parents before they leave if the children can ride these things. Also, make sure the kids all wear safety equipment such as helmets, elbow and kneepads if they do ride bikes, scooters, or skateboards. Make sure the equipment fits the children and is put on correctly. You should also ride with the children if you all go anywhere.

When you do go for a ride plan the route ahead of time. Inform the children where they are to go. Don't let them go free. Your route should be in a safe area such as a park, bike lane or a safe driveway. Do not bike in busy streets or cross dangerous intersections. You must go over safety rules and determine the kids' riding abilities before you set out. Bikes, scooters, and skateboards can be entertaining, but they can also be dangerous, plan ahead, be safe and have fun.

What about...
Strollers

Strollers are very useful especially if you are babysitting for several children or are going on a long walk. There are many different types of strollers that are designed to carry different sizes and ages of kids. Make sure the stroller that you use can carry the child. When you put a child in a stroller they should fit nicely in the sturdy seat. They should not be too cramped and there should also not be too much room where they can slide out of the stroller. You also need to secure the seat belt over the child's waist as they sit in the stroller. Strollers are also convenient to use because you can carry other items in the stroller such as a small amount of food, diapers, toys and other useful items.

You should not permit a child stand up in the stroller. You are the only one who is to push the stroller. Always keep an eye on the children in the stroller and never let go of the stroller when kids are riding.

What about...
Baby Monitors

Baby monitors are small listening devices that allow you to hear a baby from another room. One goes in the baby's room and the other stays near you. The point of the baby monitor is that you will hear the baby if he or she cries, screams or wakes up. Then you can go pick them up from their crib.

There are many different types of baby monitors so make sure you are taught how to use the one that the family has. Also, do not rely totally on the baby monitors. They may not always work, periodic checks on a sleeping child is a good idea regardless of what you hear on the baby monitor.

What about...
House Alarms

Some homes may have alarms. If they do, ask the parents to show you anything that you may need to know about them. Also ask the parents what you should do if the alarm happens to go off.

As a babysitter you can never be prepared for everything that can happen. The above items are some of the more common occurrences that you will most likely face sometime in your babysitting career. As you babysit more and more you will become more knowledgeable about how to handle different situations and there will always be situations for which you are completely unprepared. When you are faced with a "What About…" question take a minute to think about any actions you could take and the consequences of those actions. You are in charge, and if you are a good babysitter you will make good, intelligent decisions.

Chapter Nine

Just For Parents

This section is for parents who need a babysitter. Sometimes it can be just as scary for the parents to leave their children alone as it is for the babysitter to be left alone with their kids. The main rule for parents is to relax and trust yourself about your decisions. Let's face it, choosing a babysitter can be difficult. You aren't sure if the babysitter you've found is the right person for the job. You don't know if you will leave enough food, if they will find everything, if they will be safe, if they will have a good time. The list of worries that parents have can go on and on and on, but there are ways that you can lessen all of these worries by planning ahead and trusting your judgement.

When you choose a babysitter seek out a few possible choices. It is preferable to have more than one babysitter that you regularly use. This will be convenient for you if one cancels or if one moves away or does not want to babysit any longer. The best way to find babysitters is to talk to coworkers, neighbors, friends and go to the local school or community center to see if you can find potential babysitters. If you are having a hard time finding a babysitter, or a good babysitter, don't give up. There are plenty of qualified sitters out there; you just need to find the right one for you and your family.

If you find a potential babysitter you should either call them directly or talk to them in person. Suggest that their parents be with both of you for the first meeting. This will ensure your and their safety and that you are both comfortable. Conduct a mini interview. Ask the babysitter what type of experience he or she has, if they have any references, what do they like to play with children, or if they can they cook a little. Become familiar with the babysitter. Chat with them about school and everyday activities. Tell them about your family and your house. You should be able to ascertain if they are appropriate for the job from this interview. If you like them, hire them for one job and see how it goes. If you don't like them for any reason then don't hire them. You don't want to put your family or house in jeopardy. If it does not feel right, then it most likely will not be correct. Once you do hire a babysitter give them your name, number, address, kids' names and ages and the first time that they are to babysit for you. They should also give you their name, number and address. Arrange for transportation with the babysitter and close the deal with a hardy handshake and a warm smile. You now have a babysitter!

Once you find a babysitter have them come over to your house before their first job with you, if possible. This could be an hour before you are planning to leave or a week or so before you need them. Use this time to get to know the sitter better. Show them the house and tell them about any out of bounds rooms or places. Have them meet the children and the family pets. Tell them what they can and can not eat and show them where the food is. Give them any lists that you have made and review the lists with them. Make sure the babysitter and you are clear about the items on the list and everything else. It is better to tell them more than they need to know then leaving them to do things on their own or having them guess what you might want.

Once you have oriented your babysitter and it is time to leave, say a short goodbye to your children and depart. You don't want to have a long and dramatic goodbye because the kids may start crying when you leave. A new babysitter does not want to start out with a group of crying children who miss their parents. Now that you are gone you need to relax about your children. If you followed all the right steps and made all the right decisions they will be in great hands!

We are now going to go over a few main topics that parents will need to face at some point with either themselves, their kids or with their babysitter. These will hopefully help ensure that babysitting is less stressful for you and the sitter.

Trusting Your Babysitter

Trust is one of the most meaningful feelings that a parent can have for a babysitter. If a babysitter knows that the parents trust him or her then they will do a better job. They will not feel that every move they make is being scrutinized which will make them nervous and perform below their capabilities. If you do not trust a certain sitter, then don't hire them. If you hire a sitter that you don't trust, then chances are they may not do a good job because they get more nervous and can get a careless attitude. This makes a bad situation worse. You need to learn to trust your sitter and yourself with the choices that you make. It is hard to leave your kids with someone who you hardly know, but you can do it. Like most things you do for the first time, you will be a little nervous. This is normal. As you use the same babysitter over and over again, trusting them will be much easier.

Another sure-fire way to know if you picked the right babysitter is to ask your children the next day. Inquire what they did and if they had fun. If the children give you a positive response then you probably found a good sitter. If they tell you some not so good things, weigh these comments to see how serious the issues may be and if needed, give the sitter a second chance. If the kids don't like the sitter for legitimate reasons, don't ask them back. Kids will remember their babysitter for a long time. Strive to have these memories be good ones.

Laying Down The Rules

The first time you use a babysitter have them come over a half an hour to an hour before you plan on leaving. If possible have them come over a week before so they can meet the children and see the house. Give them a complete tour of the house, tell them about your neighbors, tell them who has a key to your house, show them the food, show them any areas where they are not to play, as well as anything else that you think is important. But DON'T HOUND them with too much information. You want to inform your sitter and make them feel welcome and comfortable; you don't want to scare them off with a billion rules and regulations.

As you go over the rules make sure your children hear and know the rules as well. If your kids have a different interpretation of a rule than what you tell the babysitter, this will cause more conflict. It may help to write down the most significant rules so there will not be any misunderstandings.

Pay

This is a very important issue to the babysitter. Let's face it, this is why they are working. Sometimes parents either over pay or underpay and every parent pays differently. The key is to pay your sitter the fair market value for babysitting and to pay by the hour. Talk to your friends and find out what they pay their babysitters, but you must keep in mind that the more children you have the more you should pay your babysitter. Also, if your children tend to be "difficult", you might want to pay your sitter a little more. The basic plan for paying your sitter is to use even numbers (don't count the pennies) and to pay a fair wage. Something slightly above minimum wage should be good to start. If you like the sitter, pay them a little more. The bottom line is to pay a fair price for what your sitter does for you and your family.

Cash or check, which do you pay your babysitter? The babysitter would most likely prefer cash, but a check does work as well. The draw back of cash on your part is that you may forget how much you pay a sitter for the next time. With a check you have a record. The bottom line is that either cash or check will work for most sitters, just so they can spend it as quickly as they earn it!

Safety

Many parents are obsessed with the safety of their children. In order to ensure that your child is the safest he or she possibly can be when being babysat is simple. Make the house, child, and babysitter safe. Put away potentially dangerous items around the house such as items that have jagged edges or objects that could fall on your kids. Put away expensive and irreplaceable items and those that you definitely do not want broken. Close or lock any doors that you do not want the children entering. This could include your bedroom, a storage closet or the garage. Keep all flammable and poisonous items out of your kid's reach. As you make your house safe, use common sense. It is better to take more precautions than not enough. Be sure the rules are clear and easy for the babysitter to follow and understand. Share the rules with your children and let them and the babysitter have a good time. When you leave the house, leave your kids and worries behind.

Lists

Some parents create lengthy lists for their babysitter. These lists include every minute planned out to the smallest detail. These lists appear good to you, but they do not make much sense to the babysitter. Let's face it, nothing runs as smoothly as you would like and you don't want your babysitter reading a lengthy list when they should be caring for your children. When you write a list for your sitter put the most significant information first. The babysitter will be more likely to read the top of the list and they need to know the important information. Put bedtime, mealtime, prominent phone numbers, where you will be and other necessary items at the top of the list.

If you tend to create long lists and can't help it, strive to cut it down to one side of one page, or design smaller lists that are organized by topics. This way all the information will be in one place, and there is no confusion or excuse for misinformation or misunderstanding on anyone's part.

When you do create a list, here are a few examples of what should be on it:

- where you are going
- the number where you will be or your cell phone number
- when you will return
- any instructions about the kids. For example, when is bedtime or what other activities do they need to do.
- what they can eat
- any phone numbers and names you want the babysitter to have

These items are examples of possible topics that belong on a list. The list should be simple and to the point with little room for confusion.

Scheduling

When you have chosen a babysitter give them ample notice of when you need them. You might want to write down the dates and times when they should come over and give this to the babysitter. Also, give them an honest estimate of how long you will be gone so you do not worry the babysitter or children when you do not return on time. Be considerate of your babysitter's need. If you are going to be late or your schedule changes, give them a call ahead of time. Also, call them a few days before they are supposed to babysit just to reconfirm the time and date. Teenagers can forget from time to time.

Your babysitter will most likely have a social life and would like to have ample time to arrange their schedule around their various activities. Take time to talk to your babysitter about when you will need them and when they are available. If possible, try to keep a routine going that way there will be less chance of something interfering with scheduling.

Another issue that may come up with scheduling is single parents. If you are divorced, never married, or separated make sure that the babysitter knows about anyone who may come over and claim that they need to take the children somewhere. This person could be the kid's other parent, stepparent or legal guardian. You do not want to get the babysitter stuck in a situation where someone else is claiming that your children need to go with him or her. To prevent this from happening alert everyone concerned.

Food

Have enough food in the house for the hungry teenagers who are watching your children. Make sure you show and tell them what they can eat and what they can not. Some babysitters may be shy when it comes to eating someone else's food. Make it clear to them that they should eat and show them where the utensils and dishes are found. You also need to show your kids what they can and can not eat and how much they can eat. Food is important for the children and the babysitter, make sure there is enough of it in the house.

Your Behavior

You also need to act correctly when having a babysitter over. If you are unorganized, rude, mean or scary chances are the babysitter will not stick around. You should try to be dressed and ready to go when the babysitter arrives. You, too, need to make a great first impression if you want to keep your babysitter. If a babysitter does not feel comfortable with you, your kids or your house then they most likely will not babysit for you ever again. Be pleasant, courteous and warm to your babysitter. Remember this person is going to be caring for your family and home.

Secret Word

One of the most common and worse fears for parents is that someone will attempt to kidnap their children. This fear may be heightened when they are not with their children. Parents need to designate a secret word that only their family knows. You do not tell this word to your babysitter, your neighbor or anyone else other than your children. Here is the way this works. Let's say your family's secret word is "lobster." If you are in danger or in the hospital and you want someone to bring your kids to you or take them somewhere, you tell that person that they are to tell your children the secret word is "lobster" and then your message. This way your children will know that this person is telling the truth and can be trusted even if they are a stranger. A secret family word is a very good thing to have. Remember it is a secret and should only be used when you really need it.

Laws

There are many different laws pertaining to babysitting and daycare. If you have the babysitter care for more than six children, for example, then this may legally be a daycare. If this is the case then in some states you and the babysitter need to be licensed as daycare professionals. If you are not sure about your local laws contact your police or local government and ask them what constitutes a daycare and what steps need to be taken to fulfil the requirements set forth in the law. Not every state will have the same laws. It is always better to check into any laws or regulations before you have a problem.

Hopefully you as a parent feel more comfortable with the prospect of hiring a babysitter. The most important thing that you need to do is trust the babysitter you choose and trust yourself. You know your own children better than anyone else, you know if they are difficult or easy. Try to share some of your wisdom with the babysitter beforehand. The more organized you are before the babysitter gets there, the better experience it will be for you, the babysitter, and your children.

Chapter Ten

Important Stuff

This chapter will give you an overview of many important topics that you may face as you babysit. These topics will include a wide range of first aid techniques that you need to learn. These include what to do in an emergency, how to treat major and minor injuries and other useful items. Remember most injuries that you will face while babysitting will be very minor, you still need to be prepared just in case a major injury does occur. Do not allow this section in any way turn you away from babysitting; people can get hurt in any situation doing anything. Babysitting, if made safe, is not a very dangerous job. If you would like to learn more about first aid and safety, contact your local community center for more information about first aid classes or visit your local library. They may have classes and books that will teach you more about first aid.

Getting Help

If you are faced with a very serious injury or situation and you need to call for help, this usually means calling paramedics, a family doctor, the fire department, a neighbor, your parents or the children's parents. A serious injury is an injury where the injured person is in immediate danger and could die or be permanently harmed if they do not get professional help right away. You do not want to call the paramedics if it is not a serious injury. Ninety-nine percent of the injuries that occur while babysitting will not be serious, but you need to be prepared for serious and non-serious injuries. If you are ever faced with a serious or life threatening emergency, call 911. When talking to someone from 911 or another emergency service, tell them your name, the phone number you are calling from, the address where you need help and any information about what type of help you need. The person who you are talking to may ask questions. Attempt to answer these questions the best you can. In most cases help is only a few minutes away.

First Aid

 It is inevitable that someone will probably be hurt sometime in your babysitting career. This could be the kids, the pets or even you. If something does happen the number one thing is **DO NOT PANIC**. Most injuries that occur while babysitting will not require professional medical attention, but you do need to follow the steps below for every medical emergency. These steps should be used whenever you need to deal with a medical emergency or dangerous situation.

Step one

- Survey the scene. This is the first thing you need to do when someone gets hurt. If they are in immediate danger, for instance they are in a swarm of bees or there is a fire, you may need to move the injured person despite their injuries away from the danger. But if the injured person is not in immediate dangers, leave them where they are. Moving an injured person can often cause more injuries to that person.

  If the injuries seem at all serious call 911 to request medical help. This could mean you calling the paramedics or having someone nearby call the paramedics. If you need to tend to a child, have someone else call for help. This could be an older sibling or a neighbor.

Step two

• Observe and treat the person's serious wounds first and talk to the hurt person. Make sure they are okay and conscious. Ask them their name or what day it is. You want to treat the most serious injuries first because these are the injuries that can cause the most damage. If a child has a broken leg and a small cut or scrape on their elbow, treat the broken leg first because this is a more serious injury.

When you come upon a person who is on the ground, motionless the first action you should take is tap the persons shoulder and shout to them to try to get a response. If there is no response have someone call 911, then look, listen and feel for breathing. LOOK at their chest to see if air is filling their lungs. LISTEN to their chest and mouth for breathing or short breaths. FEEL their chest for movement and their mouth for air leaving or entering their windpipe. If the person is breathing, keep them safe and tend to any wounds while you wait for paramedics.

If the person is not breathing or you can not tell if they are breathing you need to first put the hurt person on their back, supporting their head and neck. This will hopefully open their airways and get air to the hurt person's lungs. If they still are not breathing gently tilt back their head and lift their chin. Again look, listen and feel for breathing. If the injured person is still not breathing you must begin rescue breathing. Give the injured person two slow breaths into their mouth and check for a pulse. Next check and tend to any severe bleeding and other serious injuries. Then continue rescue breathing and checking for a pulse until help arrives.

Your job is to help stabilize the injured person before trained medical persons can get to the scene if the injury is serious. If it is not serious, then your job is to clean the wound and treat it with a bandage or other suitable treatment. This chapter will go over different treatments for different types of wounds and other medical issues.

Step three

- Once you have treated the wounds or injuries, look for any medical identification tags on the child. If the child does wear these tags their parents should have notified you about them. Most children do not have medical identification tags. These tags could be around their neck as a necklace or a medical bracelet. These tags will give you vital information such as the child's name and any allergies or medical conditions they have. If they do not have any tags try to recall if their parents told you they are allergic to anything, or if they have any medical conditions.

Step four

- Once the injured person has been treated you need to comfort them. Show your support to the hurt person and stay by their side.

If any injury occurs to any child or yourself when babysitting, always inform the parents no matter how small the injury. You never know if further medical attention may be needed.

Also, most families should have a first aid kit in their house. This will most likely include pain killers, bandages, moisturizers, cleaning solutions, scissors, thermometers, a first aid guidebook and other items which you may need to help save a life or to comfort an injured child. If you do not know if the family has a first aid kit, ask. If they do have one they should show you where it is and what it contains.

Bumps And Bruises

Children and especially young children frequently bump and bruise their bodies. This especially goes for youngster's heads and knees. Since many young children are unbalanced when they walk and tend to have large heads, they often bump and bruise their bodies when they fall or stumble into objects.

To treat small bruises and bumps you need to first comfort the injured child. Assure them that they will be okay and carefully check their wounds to see how serious they are. If the bruise or bump is not serious, place a cold compress or ice on the wound. Make sure you place something like a cloth or paper towel between the cold and the wound. Cold on the hurt area will help to alleviate the pain, control any swelling, and calm the child. If the bump or bruise is bleeding a great deal, turns dark purple, is very large and the child is in a great deal of pain call the injured child's parents.

Kiss-Boo-Boos

These are non-serious wounds that happen from bumping, falling or just playing. If this happens go over to the child and check for any serious wounds. If they have none then give the child a soft kiss on the hurt area and put them back on their feet. The child will wipe away the tears and continue to play.

Small Cuts

A small cut is less than a half-inch long and only bleeds a little if at all. If a small cut occurs, wash the wound with mild soap and water. Use a washcloth or a paper towel to wipe the wound, apply a bandage or other wrap over the wound to keep it clean.

Small Scrapes

Treat these in the same way as small cuts but be careful when putting on the bandage. Sometimes with scrapes the injury may be longer and wider than cuts and the bandage may hurt the injured area. Use a bigger covering for scrapes or don't put any covering over it at all if it is not bleeding or is not serious.

Large Cuts

These can be very serious. A large cut is when the wound bleeds a great deal and the child is in great pain. Seek medical attention for any serious bleeding that you can not stop after trying. To control bleeding first cover the wound with a cloth or bandage and apply direct pressure to the wound with your hand. Next elevate the wound above the injured person's heart. This will slow down the blood flow to the cut. Then cover the wound with a stronger bandage or cloth. If the wound is still bleeding apply more cloths and keep direct pressure on the injured body part. If the bleeding still can not be controlled call 911 and get professional medical attention as soon as you can. Large cuts may need stitches or other medical attention that you can not provide.

If you can get the bleeding to slow, bandage the cut firmly, but not too tightly. Make the child comfortable and call their parents.

Burns

There are three main categories of burns, first degree, second degree and third degree. A first degree burn is a small burn that involves only the top layer of skin. The skin will be red and dry and the burned area is usually very painful. This burn can occur from touching something hot such as a coffee cup of hot water. First degree burns are the most common type of burn that you will face while babysitting.

A second degree burn also involves the top layer of the skin. However, this is a more serious type of burn than first degree burns. The skin will be red and covered with blisters that can be seeping liquids from them. These burns are very painful and can also be accompanied by swelling.

A third degree burn destroys all the layers of the skin and may harm fat, muscles, and bones that are under the skin. These burns look black and charred and can be either extremely painful or almost painless if the burn destroys all the nerve endings. Third degree burns are the most serious types of burns. They can cause permanent damage to the skin.

To treat burns you need to first stop the burning. If the wound is on fire, for example, extinguish the fire. Move the victim away from the source of the burn. Secondly you want to cool the burn. You do this by placing the burned area in cool water or by placing water soaked towels over the burned area. Do not use ice or ice water on the burn, do not touch or pick at the burn and never try to use soap or other ointments on the burn. Once you have cooled the burn you will want to cover it. Use clean bandages or other cloth to loosely cover the burned area. Covering the burn helps keep dirt out of the burned area and reduces the pain. If the burn is at all serious call the children's parents.

Choking

Choking is a very common occurrence for people. Most of the time it happens during meals or while food is being consumed. Children can also choke on toys, rocks, coins and any other objects that they put in their mouths. It is very hard to tell when someone is choking. Most people think someone is choking when they are coughing or gasping for breath, this is not true. If you can cough then air is reaching your lungs and you are not choking.

Some signs of choking are grabbing one's throat or neck and struggling to speak but not being able to. If someone is choking and they are not an infant, you should ask them if they are choking. If they nod yes, you will need to clear the item out of their throat.

Helping a child who is choking

If a child (someone who is not an infant) is choking you will have to give them abdominal thrusts. Standing behind the choking person, place your fist against the abdomen just above the belly button. Grasp the fist with your other hand. Your arms will now be around the choking person. Now give quick thrusts upward. Continue to give these quick upward thrusts until the item is coughed up or until the child becomes unconscious. If they become unconscious get medical attention as quick as you can if you have not done so already.

Helping an infant who is choking

When an infant is choking place them facedown on your forearm. Their body should be angled down, with their head pointing to the floor. Give the infant five back blows with the heel of your hand between their shoulder blades. If the item is not dislodged turn the infant face up on your forearm and give them five chest thrusts on the center of the breastbone. Continue the back blows and chest thrusts until the infant begins to breathe or falls unconscious. If they become unconscious get medical attention immediately.

When a child is choking do your best to keep him or her calm. If you can not dislodge the item right away, keep on trying. Eventually you will get it out. If you can not dislodge the object seek medical attention. With choking every second counts.

Nosebleeds

Nosebleeds are very common in many children. Some causes of nosebleeds can be dryness in the nose, being hit in the nose, having objects in the nose, sinus infections, altitude changes and picking one's nose. Some nosebleeds happen for no reason at all. To treat a nosebleed check to be sure there are not any objects in the nose. If there are objects in their nose either take the object out or get medical help. If there is not an object in the nose then lean the child forward and gently pinch the lower, soft part of the nose for about five minutes. You should use a facial tissue or cloth when holding the child's nose. If the bleeding does not stop, try putting a cold compress or ice on the nose and hold the nose for ten minutes. If the nose is still bleeding then place a small amount of gauze in the nose. If the nose still bleeds get medical attention. Most nosebleeds will stop after a few minutes of treatment.

Shock

Shock is basically the body's natural reaction to something horrible or painful such as a broken bone or a large cut. A person may go into shock at any time. When a person starts to go into shock they will lay still after a serious injury. They will not be responsive to any of your actions. A person in shock will have bluish lips, gums and fingernails. They will have clammy skin and be very weak with slow, shallow breathing. And may also seem anxious, can be nauseous or overly thirsty.

If a child is in shock seek medical attention immediately. To treat a child in shock lay them down on a soft and safe surface. Do not give them water and do not overheat them. Do not move their neck or head if there are any head injuries. If there are not any neck and head injuries turn them on their side. This will insure that they do not choke and this will keep their airways open. If their head is injured keep them on their back and elevate their legs and their head slightly by putting a blanket under their head and neck. Cover the child with a light blanket to keep them from losing body heat. If a child or adult is in shock get medical attention immediately.

Seizures

A seizure is when a child or adult's body goes into convulsions and they fall down and begin to shake uncontrollably. If this happens to a child who you are babysitting, clear the area of hard or sharp objects that may be near them as they are having the seizure. Do not restrain or hold the child. Do not put anything in their mouths and keep them safe from other dangers that may be near them. If you have a blanket or pillow, try to put it under or near the child so they do not hurt themselves any further. Once the convulsions or seizure is over (they usually only last a few seconds) turn the child on their side and check to make sure they are breathing. If they are not, find medical help. If they are breathing, comfort the child and call the parents.

Checking For A Pulse

A pulse informs you that the heart is pumping blood to the injured person's body. Everybody has a pulse including yourself. To take the pulse of an infant place your fingers, not your thumb (your thumb has its own pulse), on the inside of the infants' upper arm. You will know when you find a pulse if you can feel a faint beat in the arm.

To check the pulse of older children, place two of your fingers on the child's windpipe and then move your fingers to the right or left a little. You will feel a grove in the neck where you will find the pulse.

Remember, if you do not find a pulse right away, keep trying. Sometimes it can be hard to find. You may want to find your own pulse so you will know what it feels like.

Rescue Breathing

If a child is not breathing, call 911 then check for any other wounds. If there are no neck or back injuries gently place the child on their back and open their air passageway by gently tipping back their head. Check for breathing by looking for signs of breathing, listening to their mouth, and feeling for breath. If they are not breathing securely place your mouth over the child's mouth and nose (or pinch their nose shut with you fingers) and give two slow breaths into their mouth. Breathe into their mouth until their chest gently rises. If their chest does not rise they may be choking. If they are choking you will need to clear the item that they are choking on before you continue rescue breathing. See the section about choking in this chapter.

After you have given them breathes, and their chest rose check for a pulse. If there is a pulse but the child is still not breathing, give one slow breath about every three seconds. Do this for one minute. Recheck the pulse and look, listen and feel for breathing. Continue rescue breathing as long as you can still find a pulse and the child is not breathing. Make sure you recheck the pulse every minute.

Drinking Or Eating Poison

There are many different types of poisons. Cleaning chemicals, ant traps, ink, shoe polish, weed killer, deodorant, alcohol and bleach are all examples of poisons. Noxious air, which is also a poison, can come from paint fumes, fire, or cooking gas. If there is poisonous gas in the air take the child outside or into a well-ventilated room.

If a child drinks or eats something poisonous, immediately attempt to find what it was that they drank or ate. Read the warning label on the item and follow the directions on it about ingestion. Some may say induce vomiting (make the child throw up by putting your finger gently down their throat), some may say give them water, or milk to dilute the poison, while others may say don't do anything at all. In any case where poison is involved, call poison control or 911 immediately.

Splinters

The best way to treat splinters is to prevent them. If you or the kids will be outside or walking on uneven wooden surfaces, have them wear shoes. That way they can not get splinters in their feet. Also, if they are touching rough or jagged wood have them wear gloves. If they do get a splinter you must first look at it. If it is deep do not try to remove it. Instead place the body part in warm water and soak the wound. If you do this long enough the splinter may come out by itself. If this does not work continue to soak the body part with the splinter and wait until the parents come home to decide what to do next. If you find a small splinter close to the skin attempt to pull it out if you can. You may pull it out using tweezers. If you can pull it out wash the area with soap and water, put a bandage over the wound and make sure the entire splinter is removed. If the child has a very large splinter, you may need to find medical attention.

Bites And Stings

There are many different types of stings and bites including animal bites, bee and wasp stings, snake bites and spider bites. If you find a child has been stung or bitten try to find out what injured them. Many animals may be deadly to a human if they attack them. If you do not know what bit or stung the child you may need to get them professional medical attention immediately. In most cases where a poisonous animal has bitten a human, their body will immediately show signs of trauma such as swelling, difficulty in breathing, blisters or severe pain. If these occur get medical attention as quickly as you can. Some people are extremely allergic to bee stings, therefore be sure you get him or her any medicine they may need and call the paramedics immediately. Their life may depend on it.

If the bite or sting is not life threatening (most are not) you still need to help the child. If a bee stings them, and they are not allergic, remove the stinger if it is still in the skin. You can do this by gently scraping it away from the skin with your fingernail. Once you find the bite or sting area, clean it with soap and water and apply cool water over the stung area. This will help alleviate the pain and swelling. Most stings and bites will be very painful for a few minutes and as time passes the discomfort will go away. You will want to apply a clean bandage over the area if there is bleeding. If there is not any bleeding, as the case with a bee sting, keep an eye on the stung area. If a child does get stung or bitten and it does not seem serious, keep an eye on the child. Sometimes it takes a little while for the reaction to take effect.

Allergies

Many people are allergic to various substances such as food, medicine, pollen, cats and other animals and plants. Ask the parents if the children are allergic to anything. If they are, make sure you know what these things are. Find out if they need to take a certain medicine or follow a certain plan. When you are babysitting keep an eye on the children. If they start to sneeze uncontrollably or break out in hives make sure you know what to do.

Sprains

A sprain or twist is when a body part, such as an ankle or wrist, is twisted in an abnormal fashion. The body part is not broken, but it is in a great deal of pain and may start to swell. If a child has a sprain, keep them off the injured body part and do not put the entire sprain into cold or ice water. You want to first immobilize the sprain. Place blankets, bandages and other items around the sprain so it can not be moved. However, do not bandage it too tightly because the sprain will swell. Once the sprain is immobilized then you can place a cold, wet compress or ice bag covered with a towel over the sprain. A sprain may take a few days to fully recover.

Strangers Coming To The Door

Sometimes while you babysit a stranger may approach the door. This person may be dressed in a delivery uniform, police uniform or just normal dress. If you can, peer out a window at the person and do not open the door. If you don't recognize them, or are not expecting them, do not open the door. If you do open the door, do not tell anyone that the parents are gone. Act as if you are in the family if you have to. Under no circumstance do you allow a stranger in the house no matter what story they tell you. It is better to be overly safe than sorry. Direct them to a neighbor's house if they need help.

Swimming

Swimming can be very dangerous; it is better to avoid swimming when babysitting. Most of the swimming that will be done while babysitting will be in family or community pools. Before you permit any of the kids to go in the water you must do a few things.

- It is crucial that the youngsters know how to swim. There are also different levels and abilities of swimmers. Some kids can only do the doggy paddle for a short time and then get tired while others can do a variety of strokes very well and can swim for hours. If the children don't know their level or if you are not sure, then have them stick to the shallow end.
- Find out if they tread water?
- Have they taken swimming lessons?
- Do they like the water?

If the kids do not know their ability only allow them to go in the shallow end of the pool while wearing a life jacket. You must survey, or look at, the pool area searching for any broken bottles or objects on the ground that could cause injury. Make sure there is a first aid kit and life preservers near by. Check to see how deep is the pool. You do not want a child to dive into a shallow end of the pool.

Once you have determined that the pool is safe, allow the children to  go in. They should only enter the pool by the steps or a ladder. Do not let them dive or jump into the pool until you know how deep the pool is and you know the child's swimming ability. Also, do not permit them to run around the pool. They must walk! When the children are in the pool you should watch them from outside of the pool. This is especially important if you are watching more than one child. You need to be able to see all the children all the time. You are the lifeguard, even if you are at a public pool with lifeguards; you still need to be watching the kids. If the children start to roughhouse or play dangerously, get them out of the pool. A pool is not a place for inappropriate behavior.

If a child yells for help you should first throw a floatable item in their direction. A life preserver or other floatable device should be near the pool at all times. If this does not work then use a long pole to pull the child to safety. Again, most pools should have a long pole nearby just for this use. If the child is still in danger, call 911 and then jump in the pool. It is very, very dangerous for you to attempt to help a drowning person while in the pool unless you are a trained lifeguard. When people drown they begin to panic. They may hit you or pull you under when you approach them.

If you do need to approach a drowning child, swim to their back, behind them. You do not want them to be able to grab at you and pull you under. When you do get near a drowning person grab their head gently from behind and make an effort to get them to float on their back. Once you grab their head with your arm begin to swim with the child to the side of the pool. Chances are they will relax a bit once you have them in your arms. Once you get a drowning child out of the pool get them medical attention. They may have swallowed water and could have done other damage to themselves.

You may also find yourself taking children to a lake or even to the ocean. If you do take them to a lake or the ocean you must always go in the water with the children and keep an especially close eye on them. Lakes and oceans can be unpredictable. There can be huge waves and undertows (strong currents) that pull children out into deeper water. But most lakes and oceans have beaches. You can play numerous amounts of entertaining games on the beach like building sandcastles, playing paddleball, or just relaxing on the sand. Just because you go to the ocean or lake does not mean you have to go in the water to have fun.

Swimming is a dangerous activity to do with children while babysitting, as you can tell it can be very hazardous so use your head when you and the kids are swimming. You don't want a silly mistake to ruin your enjoyment and the kid's fun.

Crib Safety

Cribs are only to be used by small children or infants when they sleep. Do not allow larger kids to climb into the baby's crib. Have the parents show you how the crib works. Many cribs have different functions such as having their sides fold down  or the pad in the crib can be removed. Try to learn as much as you can about a particular crib that the family has. You should ask what blankets the baby needs to sleep with and what else should go in the crib.

Generally infants only need one light blanket and they should not have pillows or other toys in the crib.

CPR

CPR (cardio pulmonary resuscitation) is the name for the first aid procedure that is administered when someone has heart failure or a heart attack. There are classes that you should take that will teach you CPR. Call your local community center to learn about these classes. If you are not trained in CPR you may cause more damage to the injured person if you attempt to administer it.

Some signs that someone has had heart failure are unconsciousness, they are not breathing and there is no pulse. If this happens to someone call an ambulance immediately. If you are not trained in CPR there are a few things that you can do as you wait for professional help. You can check to make sure that the child or infant is really not breathing or does not have a pulse. If they do not have a pulse or are not breathing you should begin rescue breathing. Rescue breathing is explained in this chapter. Continue rescue breathing until medical attention arrives.

Broken Bones

The most common bones people break are their arms and legs. You can usually tell a bone is broken by observing the hurt area and asking the child how got they hurt. Most broken bones will seem out of place and will be accompanied by swelling and extreme pain. Children may also break ribs, feet, fingers and other bones. If a child breaks a bone you will need to do a few things.

- Seek medical attention.
- Do not move the bone or put it in a different position. This could cause more damage. Also do not allow the child to walk if there is a chance they broke a bone.

- Check and treat other injuries such as serious bleeding before you tend to the broken bone.
- Place a bandage or other cloth over the break to keep it clean if the bone is protruding through the skin. You don't want the break to get infected.
- Comfort the child as medical professionals arrive.

It is crucial that you keep the injured person as calm as possible before help arrives. You want to keep the injured person talking and do not allow them to move the broken bone.

Fire

If there is ever a fire in the house while you are babysitting get out fast. Then call the fire department outside the home even if the fire seems small. Fire is a very strange and dangerous thing; one minute it is almost extinguished then next it is out of control. However, if you can try to fight a small fire do it. But never, never, never put your life in jeopardy. A house can be rebuilt you and the children can not. If there is a small fire on the stove you can try to turn the stove off and extinguish the fire with the lid of a pan. Never pour water over a grease fire. This will make the fire worse. Also, most homes should have a fire extinguisher. Ask the parents where it is and learn how to use it. It may save your life.

Power Outages

If the power goes out while you are babysitting, first keep the kids calm. Then turn on the flashlight that you carry in your babysitting bag. Check to see if the power is only out in the room or if the entire house is dark. If the entire house is dark and it is dark outside see if the neighbors' lights are out. If their lights are also out, then you know the whole neighborhood is probably experiencing the outage. Now attempt to find some flashlights in the house. Ask the parents before they leave if they have any flashlights. Make sure the flashlights work and the batteries are still charged. The most important thing to do in a power outage is keep the kids and yourself calm and try to find flashlights. You do not want to light candles because they can cause house fires and are very dangerous. Most phones will work in a power outage, you should call for help if you need it. Chances are a power outage will be only temporary, make the best of it and hopefully the light will come back on soon.

Plumbing Problems

Sometimes the house may have a leak, an overflowing toilet or other plumbing related problems. If this happens, do not panic. If the toilet is overflowing you need to turn off the water. This can be accomplished by looking behind the toilet near the floor for a small valve or knob. Turn this value or knob to the right until the water stops flowing. You have now turned the water off for that particular toilet. If you feel brave you can plunge the toilet with a plunger. This will help in clearing the clog. I recommend that you leave the clog there, clean up any water on the floor and continue to watch the children, and do not allow anyone to use that toilet. Your job is to watch the kids, not to be the plumber.

When it comes to leaks, try to stop the leak if you can. Once it stops, clean it up, but you do not need to try to fix the problem. Chances are you are not an expert plumber. Tell the parents when they get home what happened and what you did about it. Chances are the leaky sink, toilet or bathtub has been a problem for a while.

Lost Children

Hopefully you will never have to deal with losing a child when you babysit. The best way to avoid this is to always keep an eye on the children and set boundaries. If you are playing outside, only permit the children to stay in a certain area. If you are inside do not let the children wander away from you. If you care for the child properly they should never get lost. Most children do not want to stray too far away from their home or from you, if they are lost something may be wrong.

If you cannot locate a child you need to act quickly. First, call out the child's name to ensure they are not hiding. Then quickly search outside to see if you can find the child. Yell their name forcefully in a tone that says, "if you are hiding you better show yourself." If you still can not find the child call the police. Tell them where you are, who you are and that there is a lost child. The police will then take over from there.

Most of the time when you can not find a child they have just wandered off somewhere nearby to play. It is important to take a few breaths and quickly look for the child in the immediate area before you panic. Chances are you will find the child playing quietly by him or herself.

Child Abuse

Child abuse is when someone exploits or uses a child in a way that is harmful to that child. Child abuse is not just hurting a child physically; there is also mental abuse and other forms of abuse. At no time should you ever hit, push, swear, put down or touch a child in an inappropriate way or allow other children or people to do that to you or to a child. If you suspect someone is abusing a child you need to call the police immediately. Child abuse is a very serious crime and those who abuse children need to be removed.

Hopefully these items will help you to be prepared for any medical or other type of emergency that may happen while you are babysitting. Always remember that you are in charge and that you know what to do. You must remain calm, collective and think before you act. In most cases you will just be comforting a child when they bump their head or scrape their knee, but you may also need to save a life. Be prepared for anything.

Conclusion

Babysitting is a job that can be a part of your life for a long time. I hope this book has helped you to be better prepared to embrace this challenging and rewarding job. Babysitting is like no other job in the world. You will see the children and families that you babysit around town, you will become their friend and they will trust you. In order to do a good job use the best tool you have—yourself. Trust yourself and your judgment. While babysitting if you are ever in doubt, ask questions. Ask the parents questions, ask the kids questions and you can even ask yourself questions. There are no stupid questions. Most importantly make sure when you are babysitting that you and the children are having a good and safe time. Happy babysitting and I wish you luck. If you put your mind, heart, and soul into it you could become the best babysitter that this world has ever seen!

Babysitting Journal

This section is for you to write down any information about your babysitting jobs. You can keep important phone numbers, names, dates and notes in this section as well as using it for a babysitting journal. Write about the jobs you had, what you and the children did, any new games you learned and anything else that you desire.

TELEPHONE NUMBERS

MY PARENT'S NUMBER
home-
work-
cell phone-
pager-

MY NEIGHBOR'S NAME, PHONE NUMBER AND ADDRESS

Name:_____
Address:_____
Phone:_____

Name:_____
Address:_____
Phone:_____

Name:_____
Address:_____
Phone:_____

Name:_____

Address:_____

Phone:_____

THE NAMES, NUMBERS AND ADDRESSES OF PEOPLE I BABYSIT

Name:_____

Address:_____

Phone:_____

Name:_____

Address:_____

Phone:_____

Name:_____

Address:_____

Phone:_____

Name:_____

Address:_____

Phone:_____

Name:_____

Address:_____

Phone:_____

Name:_____

Address:_____

Phone:_____

Name:_____

Address:_____

Phone:_____

Name:_____
Address:_____
Phone:_____

Name:_____
Address:_____
Phone:_____

Name:_____
Address:_____
Phone:_____

IMPORTANT NUMBERS

Emergency—911
Police:_____
Fire Department:_____
Doctor:_____
Dentist:_____
Poison Control:_____

_____
_____
_____
_____

THE AGES AND NAMES OF THE CHILDREN I BABYSIT

Name:_____
Age:_____
Notes:_____

Name:_____
Age:_____
Notes:_____

Name:_____

Age:_____

Notes:_____

Name:_____

Age:_____

Notes:_____

Name:_____

Age:_____

Notes:_____

Name:_____

Age:_____

Notes:_____

Name:_____

Age:_____

Notes:_____

Name:_____

Age:_____

Notes:_____

Name:_____

Age:_____

Notes:_____

ANY OTHER NOTES ON THE CHILDREN AND FAMILES I BABYSIT

_____

_____

_____

_____

_____
_____
_____
_____
_____
_____
_____

WHERE AND WHEN IS MY NEXT BABYSITTING JOB

Where:_____
When:_____
Who:_____

Where:_____
When:_____
Who:_____

Where:_____
When:_____
Who:_____

Where:_____
When:_____
Who:_____

Where:_____
When:_____
Who:_____

Where:_____
When:_____
Who:_____

Where:_____

When:_____

Who:_____

Where:_____

When:_____

Who:_____

MY PERSONAL BABYSITTING NOTES

_____

_____

_____

_____

_____

_____

_____

_____

_____

_____

About The Author

Jordan Lane lives, works and plays in Southern California. You can contact the author at babysittingbible@hotmail.com.

0-595-24658-3

LaVergne, TN USA
21 July 2010
190296LV00003B/5/A